THE A-Z OF NUCLEAR JARGON

THE A–Z OF NUCLEAR JARGON

JONATHON GREEN

Routledge & Kegan Paul
London and New York

First published in 1986 by
Routledge & Kegan Paul Ltd
11 New Fetter Lane, London EC4P 4EE

Published in the USA by
Routledge & Kegan Paul Inc.
in association with Methuen Inc.
29 West 35th Street, New York, NY 10001

Set in Linotron Times, 10 on 12pt
by Input Typesetting Ltd, London
and printed in Great Britain
by T. J. Press (Padstow) Ltd
Padstow, Cornwall

Library of Congress Cataloging in Publication Data

Green, Jonathon.
The A-Z of nuclear jargon.

Bibliography: p.
1. Nuclear warfare—Dictionaries. I. Title.
II. Title: AZ of nuclear jargon.
U263.G735 1986 358'.39'0321 86–3933

British Library CIP Data also available

ISBN 0–7102–0641–0

CONTENTS

INTRODUCTION

Of all those areas of life from which we shrink, the spectre of imminent nuclear destruction is surely among the most repugnant. If discussion of death is the modern taboo, then so to a far greater extent is that of megadeath. Yet such taboos have continually to be broken. Nuclear weapons have been invented; they cannot be wished away, nor can they be ignored. And indeed they *are* talked about: willingly by those for whom peace may be, as the SAC motto has it, 'their profession' (while war remains their business); or unwillingly by the great majority of the world's population who are forced to live under this constant nuclear threat.

In 1962 the late Herman Kahn wrote his treatise on nuclear war *Thinking About the Unthinkable*: as the nuclear threat becomes ever more immediate, it is not enough merely to think about 'the unthinkable'; we have no option but to talk about it as well. In the event this is less easy than it might appear. Those who control nuclear power are generally unwilling to unveil its mysteries. If there must be a nuclear debate, then let its vocabulary be as inaccessible as possible. To this end there has evolved a massive body of obfuscation and euphemism, self-justification and political expediency, couched in acronyms, abbreviations, downright lies and daunting technicalities, all contriving to mask grim reality. The sum of such linguistic convenience is nuclear jargon.

The nature of jargon is that it contrives, with language, to make the repugnant more palatable. Simultaneously it conveys the appearance of explanation while actually intensifying the cover-up. While the nature of jargon varies as to the precise area in which it is operating, the overall concept remains constant, and jargon is never more apparent then in discussions of the nuclear forces, weapons, strategies and all-too-possible war which dominate the present and the future of the world today.

Introduction

I have attempted in compiling these 500-odd entries – varying in length from a simple definition to several hundred words – to amass as comprehensive as possible a dictionary of nuclear jargon. Such a compilation cannot, of course, magically remove the threat of nuclear war, but I would hope that its definitions will at least demystify some of the weightier areas of the 'balance of terror'. Inevitably, given the gap between compilation and publication, the march of nuclear technology will throw up some terms that I have not been able to include here. I would still like to feel that what I have included will stand as a sufficient aid in decoding all but the finest print of the nuclear debate.

The ideal lexicographer should remain disinterested. Yet it is hard when considering and attempting to unravel a complex of deliberate obfuscation not to feel some animosity towards those in whose interest it is that such complexity should stay strictly under wraps. Nor have I always found it easy as a typical representative of the mass of – with all respect to the world's anti-nuclear activists – essentially powerless individuals to appreciate the relish with which those same interests – military, governmental, academic and industrial – view the situation with so sanguine an eye and seem hell-bent on perpetuating, whether for profit, power or politics, the frightening *status quo*.

It is of little comfort that such excellent books as Andrew Cockburn's *The Threat* and Daniel Ford's *The Button* show that, for all the hi-tech sabre-rattling and jargon-heavy promises, neither side's infinitely complex nuclear scenarios may actually function as required. That the bomb, the essence of the whole apparatus, will work is never in doubt. And that we all remain threatened by that bomb is equally incontrovertible.

Today, arms control seems under increasing threat. America abandons the unratified SALT II treaty, Russia promises the inevitable tit-for-tat arms race. Messrs. Reagan and Gorbachev parade their own brand of jargon, each presenting himself as the messiah of world peace, while ritualistically decrying the efforts of the other as cosmetic, militaristic or both. Only the US Congress' belated resistance to 'Starwars' offers hope.

The concept of the 'big lie' is well-established in power politics. Tell one whopper and everything else is easy. In the world of nuclear weaponry and strategies, the single monolithic lie has not been put forward; no one is pretending, for instance, that the missiles are carrying confetti. Yet the agglomeration of smaller lies, encapsulated in all those linguistic exercises that make up the jargon of nuclear war, makes for that larger untruth.

This compilation does not aim to crusade. Its entries are not intended to lay bare some hitherto defended truths, but they are designed to clarify certain obscurities which those who coined them are quite happy to leave obscure. It is not a tract but a dictionary and as such has attempted to fulfill one simple task: to explain what things mean. Why the language of an issue so fundamental to the existence of an entire planet should be so arcane, and should require such deciphering, remains, of course, open to discussion.

Jonathon Green

A

A ring the circle of complete destruction that surrounds the epicentre of the explosion of a nuclear device. The A ring is an area surrounding **ground zero** with an **overpressure** exceeding 11 psi. Such a degree of blast will cause an estimated 85 per cent of deaths, assuming no adequate shelter protection.
See also **B ring, C ring**

ABC warfare acronym for Atomic, Biological and Chemical warfare. Battlefield strategies dependent on the full range of weaponry available to modern armies: atomic and latterly nuclear armaments; toxins developed from natural substances, including micro-organisms such as anthrax, which can cause disease and death in human, animal and plant life; artificial agents, including nerve gases, which can be used to disable and kill the enemy.
See also **CW, integrated battlefield, NBC warfare**

ABM acronym for anti-ballistic missiles. ABM technology – the extension of anti-aircraft gunnery into the missile age, developed in parallel with the superpower researches into the offensive missiles themselves. The USA used their Nike-Zeus and Nike-X missile systems, latterly refined as Sentinel and Safeguard, to set up a fledgling ABM system in 1956. The Russians, starting in the 1940s, were able in 1962 to install a primitive system around Leningrad. By 1964 the sophisticated Galosh ABMs were in place around Moscow and, inevitably, the US response was to upgrade their own attempts to shoot down the enemy missiles before they could explode. In 1969 President Nixon ratified a substantial increase in US ABM development. ABM systems can best be overcome by simple saturation – too many missiles to be shot down in the available time – and the appearance of **MIRVs** in the 1960s as the perfect means of such overkill lent weight to those who saw the ABM as creator of a 'defensive' arms race that would simply mirror the traditional 'offensive' struggle. The **SALT I** talks of 1972 ratified the 'Treaty on the Limitation of Anti-Ballistic Missiles'. This was to last indefinitely and was intended to end any 'defensive' arms race; each side would be allowed only two ABM systems – one to protect the respective capital city and the other to protect a single **ICBM** installation. Two years later the facility was cut to one system only. Ironically, the MIRVs, which had been created to nullify the ABMs, now had no real place in the arsenals except, as it turned out, to fuel further efforts towards parity and then superiority in the acquisition of this new brand of offensive weapon. President Jimmy Carter persisted in holding to the ABM Treaty. Ronald Reagan made it clear that the 1972 accord was 'an historical mistake' which 'ties our hands for ever'. As long as the **MAD** scenario was generally acceptable, any efforts to defuse the arms race seemed sensible. In the mid-1980s, touting the Pentagon's belief in a 'winnable' nuclear war, President Reagan felt no such restraint. To this end Reagan has looked for ways to escape the restrictions of SALT I. Many of the current technological advances, such as **MARV**ed warheads and plans for energy-beam and laser weapons, tend not towards the defensive uses that are claimed for them but towards the destabilising of the strategic balance. The current **Star Wars** plans are in effect a super-ABM system, based on the premise that only American technology can, and should, be permitted to safeguard world peace. On the offensive front, the **MX** missile is said to require some form of ballistic missile defence (**BMD**), which would be unlawful under the ABM treaty as it stands. As of May 1985 the US is trying for a double attack on the ABM treaty. On the diplomatic front the negotiators have dragged out a clause from 1972 which provides for the scrapping of the ABM treaty should an arms treaty of more general import not have been concluded within five years of the initial signature. President Carter chose to extend the ABM rules, but President Reagan wants out. Simultaneously the Pentagon claims that the Soviets have continually and extensively cheated on the ABM treaty – indeed, both parties have cheated throughout by continuing with R&D programmes on ABM systems that, under the treaty, could never be deployed – and that, in this case, the US has every justification for going its own way. To underline this the

US is engaged in compiling as large as possible a list of these contraventions. All of this, from the Soviet point of view, is construed as aggression. The US, it is considered, is not aiming at defence, inside or outside the ABM treaty; what 'Star Wars' and its allied advances really imply is a new US initiative towards first-strike capability. Such beliefs, which are shared by the more doveish of US experts, can only undermine the fragile nuclear peace that still restrains the superpowers.

See also **ASAT, BMD, ICBM, star wars**

absolute dud a nuclear weapon that fails to explode on target.

acceptable casualties the percentage of casualties that can be suffered in combat when forcing a retreat, defeat or similar reversal. Applicable to all levels of combat up to nuclear exchange, at which point civilian casualties have to be taken into account. What is acceptable to the strategic planners seems, fortunately, to vary between the paper studies of the US think tanks and the possibility of an actual war. In 1961, when East–West tensions were exacerbated by the building of the Berlin Wall, and the US still possessed a definite nuclear superiority, it was suggested that a first strike attack might now be feasible; according to the planners, the Soviet retaliation would kill at least 20 million Americans. This, they had computed, was acceptable. Fortunately the politicians and military were less sanguine. It is to be hoped, in an age of infinitely greater military capability, that the chilly assumptions of the number-crunching hardware will still be balanced by flesh and blood restraint.

See also **megadeath**

ACDA acronym for Arms Control and Disarmament Agency. The ACDA was set up in 1961 by the US; it had four aims: (1) 'The conduct, support and coordination of research for arms control and disarmament policy formation'; (2) 'The preparations for and management of US participation in international negotiations in the arms and disarmament field'; (3) 'The dissemination and coordination of public information concerning arms control and disarmament'; (4) 'The preparation for, operation of, or, as appropriate, direction of US participation in such control systems as may become part of

US arms control and disarmament activities.' Despite these aims, it was soon apparent that the Administration's view of the Agency, under a succession of right-wing, hard-line directors, was more interested in sabotaging real progress in talks than encouraging it. Fred Ikle was appointed by President Ford to ensure that Henry Kissinger's efforts to make a real breakthrough on **SALT II** in 1976 were wasted. When President Carter appointed Paul Warnke to the job, he met overwhelming opposition from those who saw him as too soft on Moscow; his appointment, said one far-right critic, was 'like choosing a boll weevil to head the Department of Agriculture'. President Reagan's director, Eugene Rostow, the veteran law professor, elder statesman and leading member of the right-wing lobby group The Committee for the Present Danger, seemed ideal for the White House's posture on arms control. In the event Rostow moved from a hard-line to a far more flexible position. His enemies in the Bureau of Politico-Military Affairs (the State department's in-house mini-Pentagon) found it simple to persuade Reagan to sack him. He went, aggrieved and unbowed, in January 1981. He was replaced by Kenneth Adelman, a 36-year-old neoconservative whose appointment met severe resistance in the Senate before it was ratified. Adelman lacked the clout a Rostow could muster and the ACDA, by no means popular with the Administration, faded further from influence. Its staff was cut by a quarter, its research budget by a half, there were lengthy delays in the choosing of senior officials; with justification a writer in *Foreign Affairs* (Summer, 1983) declared 'the ACDA is in no position to fulfil its responsibilities effectively'.

active defence the use of weapons systems – both conventional and nuclear – to defeat enemy troops; the implication is that the enemy will have made the first hostile move.
See also **point defence**

ADCOM acronym for Aerospace Defence Command.
See also **NORAD**

AFAP acronym for artillery-fired atomic projectile.
See also **tactical nuclear weapons**

AFSATCOM acronym for Air Force satellite communications system. A USAF communications system which, while it has no actual satellite dedicated to itself, works by mounting its transponders on other satellites. AFSATCOM has been in operation since 1974, providing the Air Force with communications between command posts and missile launch centres, with receivers aboard bombers, reconnaissance aircraft and submarines. Part of the overall US **C³I** complex. By 1986 the USAF will have spent an estimated $1.5bn constructing some 920 AFSATCOM terminals. Once the programme is complete, AFSATCOM-capable planes will be able to obtain and report instant updates on their position, enemy movements, etc., and will thus fulfil its mission to provide command and control over the whole range of strategic bombers, flying command posts, silo-based missiles and **TACAMO** aircraft, coming into its own when hostile jamming efforts or nuclear blackouts are severe.
See also **FLTSATCOM, MILSTAR**

AGI acronym for auxiliary gatherer intelligence/aliens gathering intelligence. The Russian 'trawlers' and similar vessels that are used to track NATO fleets or anchor conveniently near land-based military installations.

air breather a jet or rocket engine that requires the intake of air for the combustion of its fuel.

air burst a nuclear explosion that is detonated sufficiently far above the ground to ensure that none of the fireball actually touches the ground and thus none of the effect of the explosion is dissipated by local geographical factors such as irregular contours. For a 1 MT bomb the explosion would have to be centred some 1 km above the ground to keep the fireball from touching the earth. An air burst ensures the maximum production and dissemination of radiation in the immediate areas of the detonation, but since it does not create a crater, there is no production of the long-term fallout which accompanies a ground burst; even the effects of the radiation that the air burst does cause are mainly academic, since the heat and blast that accompany the explosion will be the cause of maximum destruction and casualties. The air burst is designed

for use against any large-scale concentration, notably large cities or industrial areas.
See also **ground burst**

air defence warning conditions
(1) yellow – attack by hostile aircraft and/or missiles is probable; hostile aircraft and/or missiles are *en route*; unknown aircraft and/or missiles suspected to be hostile are *en route* towards, or within, an air defence sector or division.
(2) red – attack by hostile aircraft and/or missiles is imminent/ in progress; hostile aircraft and/or missiles are within an air defence division/sector or in its immediate vicinity, with high probability of entering that division/sector.
(3) white – attack by hostile aircraft and/or missiles is improbable (this may be issued before or after yellow or red conditions).

airborne alert the policy of maintaining a bomber force permanently in the air around the clock in order to make for a more speedily launched offensive and to save planes from being destroyed on the ground. This was abandoned by the USAF, its chief advocate, in 1968, by which time the USA's main defences were entrusted to missiles, but it is put into operation on the declaration of any level of crisis alert.

ALCM acronym for air launched cruise missile.
See also **cruise missiles, GLCM, SLCM**

alert crew
(1) five-man USAF teams who man the Strategic Air Command (**SAC**) missile launch facility at Offutt Air Force Base and the equivalent posts in the **Cover All** flying command post.
(2) the SAC bomber crews who ranked second in excellence and skill to the 'select crews'. These categories were originated in 1951 by **SAC** commander General Curtis LeMay.

anticipatory reaction a surprise attack.
See also **anticipatory retaliation, pre-emptive strike**

anticipatory retaliation a surprise attack.

See also **anticipatory reaction, massive retaliation, preemptive strike**

arc light a bomb strike delivered by a B-52 bomber. The flash and explosion of the massive payload gives an exceptionally bright light.

area defence the ability to defend a large proportion of one's country; in a US nuclear scenario, this means the protection of cities. Under the 1972 ABM treaty, area defence against nuclear attack was outlawed, and ABM sites were restricted first to two and latterly to one only. In the event the US has no area defence, and the Soviets have only thirty two Galosh missiles surrounding Moscow. The new plans for US ballistic missile defence, while contravening the ABM treaty if they are put into effect, will concentrate on defending ICBM sites rather than the vulnerable cities.

See also **point defence**

ASALM acronym for advanced strategic air-launched missile. A development of the ALCM initiated in the mid-1970s. This bomber-launched missile was designed to skim the ground for long distances at supersonic speed. It had fins like a rocket but because of its speed did not, unlike cruise, require wings to stay in flight. ASALM was intended to destroy hostile aircraft which in turn sought to attack cruise missiles, and to destroy anti-aircraft missile sites (also threatening incoming cruise) as well as penetrating to strategic targets. ASALM was to be powered by a rocket/ramjet solid-fuelled engine in which the rocket-fuel motor-casing doubles, once it has put the missile into supersonic speed, as a ramjet combustion chamber. It would reach its target using **TERCOM** guidance, backed up by some extra facilities. In November 1977 ASALM was put forward two years, rescheduled for possible service in 1985. In the event, the ASALM programme seemed to go into abeyance in 1981, at the same time as the news of developing **stealth** technology became public. Some believe that ASALM development may have been redirected to a new strategy – the penetrating of enemy airspace at high altitudes and great speeds. At the same time as ASALM 'vanished', there were rumours of a new hypersonic cruise missile, flying at 100,000 feet and at several times the speed of sound. It would be powered by a supersonic rocket, the SCRAMJET, using liquid hydrogen fuel. *See also* **cruise missiles**

ASAT acronym for anti-satellite weapons. A variety of conventional, nuclear, electronic and laser weaponry designed or intended for the destruction of hostile communications satellites or to defend against hostile ASAT weapons. The first 'test' of an ASAT weapon was an accident; when in October 1962 the USAF and Atomic Energy Commission carried out a high-altitude nuclear test (code-named STARFISH) it was found that the explosion fatally damaged a number of orbiting satellites, none of which were directly in line with the explosion but which were wrecked by the massive dose of high-energy electrons released into their paths. In 1963, alerted by rumours of a Soviet 'orbital bomb', President Kennedy authorised an 'active anti-satellite capability' and between 1964 and 1967 the US Army launched a number of anti-ballistic missiles (on Nike-Zeus rockets) as 'interim' ASAT weapons. In March 1964 the USAF commenced a series of tests – code-named SQUANTO TERROR – using a Thor missile to project a fake warhead (live tests above the ground had been prohibited in the Limited Test Ban Treaty, 1963) from Johnson Island, SW of Hawaii, some 700 miles high and 1,500 miles downrange. Success was determined by an 'explosion' 5 miles or less from the target – a piece of US space debris or a dead satellite – and in the sixteen exercises up to 1968 the distance was cut to nine-tenths of a mile. Although orbiting nuclear weapons were banned in 1967, the SQUANTO TERROR launchers were not dismantled until 1975, however obvious it was that, were the system used, the damage would not be restricted to Soviet satellites alone. Russia started ASAT tests in 1968, concluding twenty exercises by 1982 and satisfying the Pentagon by 1980 that a Soviet system was 'operational'. Soviet ASAT tests give some idea of the system. A target satellite is launched at an angle of 62–6 degrees at ranges of 340–1,200 miles; days or even weeks later the interceptor is sent up, mounted on a heavyweight SS-9 missile. It reaches the target, staying in a lower orbit, then, on command, 'pops up' to the same orbit. As it passes the target satellite it explodes into a shower of high-speed metal fragments; an attack is estimated as 'successful' if the explosion comes at anything under 8 km from the target. While the system may well work, there are drawbacks: the real ceiling is nearer 600 miles than 1,200 miles and there are virtually no US satellites of major importance that can be reached at an angle of 62–6 degrees, and the one that does flies at some 1,000 mph faster than its Soviet assailant. The guidance system of the SS-9 has also been seen as wanting in accuracy.

US ASAT efforts are currently concentrated in a number of fields, the first being the most concrete – the Prototype Miniature Air-Launched System (**PMALS**) which centres on the Miniature Homing Intercept Vehicle (**MHIV**). The system, packed into a custom-made two-stage missile some 18 feet long and weighing 2,600 lb, can be launched in mid-air from the wing of an F-15 fighter. It first picks up the infra-red emissions from a satellite and then projects the MHIV, spinning twenty times per second, into the path of the satellite. The combined speeds of the satellite and the projectile will destroy both on impact. Far more flexible than the Soviet system – Boeing Aerospace have designed a kit that can fit any F-15 with PMALS capability in six hours – it too is restricted. The air launch gives it flexibility and surprise – there is no traceable rocket launch – and the F-15's guidance system has been modified to ensure the accuracy of the PMALS missile in flight, but so small a launch platform means its range remains short. Greater range could be achieved with a larger launcher, but this in turn would sacrifice its flexibility.

PMALS is controlled from the **SPADOC** headquarters in Cheyenne Mountain, Colo., which uses the **SPADATS** surveillance system for targeting. If everything goes to plan a hostile interceptor can be spotted, an F-15 with PMALS activated and the intruder destroyed within 45 minutes. To ensure the efficiency of the system, SPADATS uses the highly sensitive Ground-Based Electro-Optical Deep Space Surveillance (**GEODSS**) and **TEAL AMBER** systems to spot hostile satellite activity instantly. For purely defensive purposes the simplest ploy is, acting upon information of hostile activity, to move a satellite into a different orbit; the USAF Space Division is researching methods of achieving this. The efficacy of such evasive action will work, but not if the hostile satellite possesses sensors that home in on any infra-red emissions, irrespective of orbit.

A variety of non-nuclear ASAT technology is being considered: space mines that 'track' a satellite for years, possibly disguised as 'innocent' communications satellites, waiting to be triggered on command; the use of radio frequency or electromagnetic pulses to jam satellite–ground communications without harming the actual satellite is feasible; laser weaponry has been mooted (*see also* **SBL**), but the technology involved is so complex, so delicate and, for the purposes envisaged, would need to be so large, that it might well be more vulnerable than the satellites it was intended to disable. Rumours of a Russian ground-based laser weapon persist, but the one recorded 'blinding' of a US satellite was found to stem from a gasfield fire, not some Soviet superweapon.

See also **ASAT treaty**

ASAT Treaty acronym for anti-satellite weapons treaty. The US and USSR started meetings on the possibility of limiting the militarisation of space in 1978. Two further meetings followed, the second being in Vienna in June 1979. A fourth was planned for February 1980, but the invasion of Afghanistan in December 1980 put paid to that. The new Reagan administration saw no purpose in re-opening the talks. On the one hand they repudiated any of President Carter's arms control agreements – such agreements, it was posited, were the cause of the current American inferiority in the arms race – while on the other it was felt that as long as **PMALS** was still unproven, there was nothing to negotiate about. Once PMALS was tested satisfactorily, the US would have superiority in ASAT weaponry, and could hardly benefit by volunteering to limit it. The US is also convinced that verification of treaties covering space weapons is virtually impossible – the Russians could and would cheat. The two areas in which such treaties might be useful, thus saving billions of tax dollars and giving the chance to declare space off-limits to warfare, seem to carry little appeal to the two authorities – the government and the military – who might be empowered to make such restraints practical.

See also **ASAT**

ASMS acronym for advanced strategic missile systems.

Formerly ABRES – advanced ballistic re-entry systems. An all-service research programme administered by the USAF to develop an advanced precision version of the Manoeuvrable Re-entry Vehicle (MARV). This development of the basic MARV will rely on the working of twin flaps for navigation (rather than the crooked nose and shifting weight guidance system that preceded it) and will incorporate sensors to guide the vehicle onto its target accurately. This advanced MARV, conceived in 1975, was originally named the Precision Guided Re-entry Vehicle (PGRV) and later renamed the Advanced MARV (AMARV). Its function is to evade hostile interceptors while maintaining its own precision accuracy. The ASMS programme has been divided into three phases: the first, the feasibility study, is complete; the second and third, the building and testing of prototype AMARVs and the development of a radar-based homing sensor, are still in progress in the mid-1980s. AMARV technology will possibly be integrated with the **NAVSTAR** global positioning guidance system, to achieve a **CEP** of only 30 feet. The system has naturally been seen as enormously destabilising the strategic balance. A warhead that can bob and weave its way past interceptors and onto a target adds massively to the threat posed by its user. To Russian eyes, the AMARV confirms the theory that the US is working not for defence but for full first-strike capability. At least in technology, and in a worst case view, strategically, the Soviets will respond to what they perceive as a major new threat posed by AMARV deployment.

See also **MARV**

assured destruction the policy of 'assured destruction' (later 'mutual assured destruction' (**MAD**)) typified US–Soviet nuclear relations in the 1960s and, for all the theories of 'winnable', 'limited' wars, is still a major ingredient of the nuclear standoff that dominates superpower policies in the 1980s. While American superiority was still assumed, Eisenhower's 'massive retaliation' – 'Whatever they do, we shall blast them from the face of the earth' – held good. Russian advances, epitomised in the SS-6 rocket that not only could put a Sputnik into orbit but could also deliver an ICBM, forced a new US posture. US Secretary of Defense, Robert MacNamara, outlined the concept of **flexible response** in 1963 – in effect a fine-tuning of massive retaliation. In 1964 a further refinement was introduced, assured destruction. 'Such a strategy requires a force considerably larger than would be needed for a limited cities-only strategy . . . it should be large enough to ensure the destruction . . . of the Soviet Union, Communist China and the Communist satellites as national societies . . . and, in addition, to destroy their war-making capability so as to limit, to the extent practicable, damage to this country and to our allies.' In the event, this policy was simply defined as holding the civilian, and particularly urban, populations of each country to ransom. For the rest of the decade both superpowers concentrated on creating massive 'city-busting' armouries. Eighty per cent of US missiles were targeted on Russian cities, and it was assumed that a successful strike would destroy 25 per cent of the Russian people and 50 per cent of her economic infrastructure. It was also assumed that the Russians were capable of a similar assault. As Senator Eugene MacCarthy put it in 1968, 'We have a three to one advantage over the Russians which I understand means we have the potential to kill all the Russians twice and they have the potential to kill us one and a quarter times.' The military remained sanguine. 'Soft' human targets were far more easily devastated than 'hardened' silos, and generals talked of 'winning' such an exchange. There was also an added bonus for the USA; a stalemate with the Russians in the international arena meant that the war in Vietnam could be left heading the foreign policy agenda. In the end this arms race did create demands for arms control. Even as the policy took hold, there had been five US-inspired peace initiatives between 1963–8. The new President, Richard Nixon, capitalised on these at the **SALT I** talks held in Helsinki from 1969–72. Yet assured destruction remained US policy until 1974, when a new generation of weapons and strategies changed the form, if not the content, of the nuclear standoff. Ironically, a *status quo* that depends on two equally strong adversaries living in peace by maintaining an admittedly uneasy '**balance of terror**' might remain the most pragmatic approach to the post-Hiroshima world. It has only been the hardline military–industrial–academic consensus that has striven to pursue the open-ended arms race that in turn refuses to be curbed by attempts at control. Global destruction has been assured for many years; the continuing technological embellishments have become vital not for the nuclear arsenals but for the many interested parties.

See also **finite deterrence, flexible response, MAD, minimum deterrence**

ASW acronym for anti-submarine warfare. Anti-submarine warfare, the single most essential element of NATO sea policy, and the one in which the West has the most commanding lead, comprises all the active and passive measures to reduce or nullify the effectiveness of hostile submarines. To track the **SSBN**s (undersea weapons platforms for nuclear missiles) and the hunter-killer subs that wage the undersea battles, ASW concentrates on detection, precision location, identification and (as yet in theory) destruction. To this end are used submarines, surface vessels, helicopters, satellites, specially equipped aircraft and underwater listening devices (hydrophones). While nuclear submarines are relatively 'quiet', it is possible for sophisticated microphones to pick up their 'signature' – the sound of the propeller, the thermal and ultra-violet radiation disruptions and the trail of dead micro-organisms left in their wake. The USN maintains a worldwide undersea network of sound surveillance systems (**SOSUS**) – submarine microphones strung in arrays across the various 'choke points' through which the essentially landlocked Russian navy is forced to pass on its way to deeper and wider oceans. In parallel to these is the **CAESAR** network, operating surveillance towed array systems (**SURTASS**) in which sonar arrays are towed through the water over wide sweeps of pre-arranged areas. Information from both networks, plus aerial and surface vessel surveillance, is all processed at ASWCCCS (Anti-Submarine Warfare Centre Command and Control Systems) in the US. The drawback of SOSUS is that, being static, it cannot track a submarine once it has registered its passage; there is also the time-lag between a sounding and the action taken by ASWCCCS. Research continues into the analysis and decoding of all undersea sounds, isolating submarines from the organic life. The Russians lag behind in ASW, as much hampered by the vast and accessible US coastline as in lack of technological advance. In the **START** talks they suggested the designation of 'ASW-free zones', but the US rejected this unconditionally. Unable to maintain tracking systems, the Russians have allegedly chosen to target ICBMs on supposed SSBN support centres.

As well as the sophisticated tracking and surveillance systems, the US Navy carries two tactical nuclear missiles designed for sea-to-sea use. Frigates, destroyers and cruisers carry the ASROC RUR-5A, an unguided, range-controlled single-stage missile, which carries a nuclear depth charge up to 7 miles. US submarines carry the SUBROC UUM-44A, a missile launched from submarine torpedo tubes, carrying a warhead of up to 5 KT yield over 35 miles. Both these weapons are scheduled for replacement by the anti-submarine warfare stand-off weapon (**ASW/SOW**) which will have a range of up to 90 miles, a more sophisticated guidance system, and which will deliver a nuclear-tipped depth bomb, effective against the most modern and deep-diving Soviet submarines. While destruction of enemy submarines remains theoretical, the US is also developing the MK 48 torpedo; wire-guided and acoustically sensitive, it can make repeated attacks on a target. The UK Sting Ray lightweight torpedo, rushed to the Falklands fleet in 1982 although still under development, has onboard sonar and digital computer guidance.

The Soviet fleet, while eschewing attempts at ASW surveillance, does have some anti-submarine weapons: the SS-N-14 (Silex) is the equivalent to ASROC, using either a homing torpedo or a nuclear depth charge, and is carried mainly on cruisers; the SS-N-15, the equivalent to SUBROC, is carried on Victor-class submarines and delivers a nuclear depth charge at a range of up to 15 miles. The Soviets also possess the FRAS-1 unguided anti-submarine rocket, 15 KT nuclear torpedoes and a variety of 5–20 KT nuclear sea mines.

See also **ASW/SOW**

ASW/SOW acronym for anti-submarine warfare stand-off weapon. A version of the Tomahawk **SLCM** designed to be fired from a submarine's torpedo tube or from a surface ship's launcher. This missile would fly towards a designated hostile submarine within its range of 300 miles and then drop a remotely-guided lightweight (REGAL) torpedo by parachute. This torpedo would release into the water an acoustic array, complete with computer and sonar transmitter, which would sink to a preset depth. Once the enemy submarine is spotted by the array, the transmitter and computer would combine to target the torpedo on the submarine. ASW/SOW is scheduled for deployment in the mid-1980s.

See also **ASW**

atomic music top secret communications between UK and US concerning mutual control and engineering of nuclear missiles.

attack options varieties of methods and targets available to a US President under the **SIOP**. These include: MAOs (major attack options, an all-out retaliatory attack); SAOs (selected attack options, on only certain specific targets); LNOs (limited nuclear options, aimed specifically at fixed enemy military or industrial centres); RNOs (regional nuclear options, aimed to destroy the military command of a given area). In addition to these is one special category which covers a US pre-emptive strike (the previous options all assume response rather than initiation) – LOW/LUA (launch on warning/launch under attack, all out retaliation on the warning or in the event of an attack). LOW assumes sufficient computer-based warning (maximum 30 minutes) and assessment of impact points for US ICBMs to be launched before they were destroyed in their silos. The essential immediacy of LOW/LUA response, coupled with its dependence on an increasingly complex (and thus vulnerable to more and more errors) electronic surveillance and warning system, makes both options highly open to internal faults that may be literally beyond human control. The proposed 'star wars' weaponry, if it materialises as envisaged, is likely to require a program so sophisticated and a computer so massive that, even if such a system were to be successfully put into operation, it would have to be self-policing since it would transcend human ability in its complexity. Add this to the **C³I** computers, themselves challenging human operators, and the LOW/LUA option becomes increasingly dangerous. Computers continually alter, but one factor remains; once ICBMs are launched, under no matter what option, they cannot be recalled.

attrit abbreviation for attrition. In the nuclear context, simply another euphemism for death. The nuclear battlefield computes deaths in 'attrits per second'. The attrit is central to NATO

A

thinking about the presumed invasion of Europe by Warsaw Pact forces sited along the border between the Germanies. This has created the 'attrition mindset', an obsession with numbers – of troops, tanks, aircraft and *materiel* – that sets the pattern for any calculations about future ground battles. It leads to a rigidity of tactical thought that ignores the imponderables, especially the role of human beings on these technological battlefields.

austere cantonment a military installation set up by a superpower in a client state, 'prepositioned' there for the purpose of waging some successful **austere war**. The theory behind such establishments is the countering of Russian colonial ambitions; if the Russians choose to launch attacks other than on CONUS (South-West Asia is a currently favoured environment), US Rapid Deployment Forces should be ready to challenge them. Other flashpoints include Africa, Central America, South America and the Caribbean. The US is currently constructing cantonments (originally used for the permanent British Army garrisons in India) in Egypt, Oman, Kenya, Somalia, Diego Garcia and the Azores.

austere wars the concept of winnable nuclear wars, fought between the client states of the superpowers, and thus kept both geographically distant from the US and considered, for all the use of nuclear weapons, as controllable by the powers. A concept developed by US Secretary of State Caspar Weinberger in *The DoD Annual Report to the Congress*, fiscal year 1984. To pre-create bases for these wars, the US is funding and building a series of **austere cantonments** around the world.

averager a proponent of one of the two opposing viewpoints on the hazards of nuclear radiation. The averager looks at the general population and assesses the average effects on the basis of the millions of people affected.

See also **hot spotter**

AWACS acronym for Airborne Warning And Control System. An aircraft-carried early-warning system. By working high over the earth AWACS, operating from converted Boeing 707s, has a far greater range than a static ground-based radar. AWACS replaced the earlier EC-121 radar surveillance planes, deployed by the US to cover the gaps in the **BMEWS** network as from January 1979. The supply of these sophisticated aircraft to Saudi Arabia continues to rankle in Middle East circles. The RAF is still tied to the Nimrod aircraft, dating from the 1950s, for its airborne warning system. The replacement for the Nimrod – Ministry of Defence planners rejected the AWACS – has yet to achieve satisfactory test ratings. Vastly over-budget, it seems that this attempt to sidestep American influence has rebounded expensively on the British government and taxpayer.

See also **NORAD**

AWDREY acronym for Atomic Weapons Detection Recognition and Estimation of Yield. Developed in the 1960s to detect nuclear explosions through the heat and electromagnetic pulses (**EMP**) from the explosion. AWDREY can detect an explosion at least 70 miles away. The instrument exists to detect bombs that explode without warning; unlikely though this seems, such an explosion could occur in the UK if the attack came, not from Russia, but from 'the wrong way', thus avoiding the **BMEWS** installation at Fylingdales in Yorkshire.

B

B ring a circle around **ground zero** in which the overpressure registers at between 6–11 psi. In this ring there would be an estimated 40 per cent deaths without adequate shelter protection.

See also **A ring, C ring**

B1-B bomber the B-1 bomber was conceived as a replacement for the B-58 and B-70 high altitude bombers (neither of which were built). By 1976, when a Brookings Institute paper concluded that there was no military advantage to be gained from deploying the B-1 fleet (originally envisaged at 244 aircraft, later scaled down to 150), the project had run far over budget and was bedevilled by a variety of technical problems. Not only did the fuselage develop major cracks but the plane was unable to exceed Mach 1.6 without suffering severe vibrations. In an attempt to cut the escalating budget the development had been subject to a number of 'engineering tradeoffs' – cuts in quality – such that the plane lacked the crew's escape module and a good deal of the vital heat-suppression facilities that were necessary to mask the aircraft from hostile infra-red scanners. Representative Thomas J. Downey condemned the B-1 as 'a military-industrial welfare programme rather than an efficient weapon' and President Carter cited the B-1 as 'an example of a proposed system which should not be funded and which would be wasteful of taxpayer dollars'. In 1977 he suspended the B-1 programme, sending Rockwell shares plummeting and savaging employment in the California defence industry. For those who saw any high-altitude penetrative bomber as anachronistic in an era of missiles, the move was correct. In the general antipathy towards Carter and all his works, Ronald Reagan reactivated the B-1 programme, ordering 100 B1-B bombers in 1981. The next model would be fully equipped with sophisticated electronic systems to counter

Soviet air defences and would be armed with sixteen gravity bombs, eight internally mounted **ALCMs** and sixteen external **SRAMs**. Its combat radius would be 9,600 km. Any doubts as to the need for such technology were dispelled by the September 1983 shooting down of a Korean Airlines jumbo. Reagan forced through massive funds for the B1-B in the face of this supposedly unanswerable demonstration of Soviet air defensive power. That experts on the Red Army claimed that such fears were pure fantasy and that the PVO (Protivo-vozdushnaya protiva) is simply not that efficient was discounted, as was the opposite view, that no bomber, however well equipped, could hope to penetrate Soviet airspace. The full B1-B fleet should be on station by 1988 and by the 1990s the B1-B will be used as a vital cruise missile launcher.

backchannel secret lines of communication held open between US and Soviet negotiators during arms control talks. Such negotiations are kept secret from the public and often from junior members of the negotiating team; their intimacy is intended to improve relations and create compromises along which the negotiations can proceed. Highly popular with Henry Kissinger, who used his own knowledge of nuclear weaponry and his personal contacts with Soviet leaders to speed up **SALT I** and **SALT II**, such off-the-record confidences have been a feature of all major negotiations, including the 'walk in the woods' taken by Paul Nitze and Soviet Ambassador Yuli Kvitsinsky in the **INF talks** of 1982. The beauty of such backchannels is that if they succeed both sides can claim credit and if they fail they need never have happened at all. The main problem is to coordinate them with the progress of the mainline talks, which will inevitably be tied far more closely to the state of national rhetoric. 'Backchannel' is taken from the CIA's clandestine cable network that runs in parallel with the official communications systems linking Washington with its embassies abroad.

Backfire the Russian Tupolev TU-22M/TU-26 large swing-wing twin jet supersonic bomber. Backfire has been developed to overcome flaws in the TU-22 Blinder, and remained in development for nearly a decade before deployment in 1974. The fleet of 210 Backfires, with thirty more under production each

B

year, can fly up to 5,000 miles (extendable with aerial refuelling, and thus capable of reaching the US). Most Backfires are deployed for anti-shipping or theatre nuclear activities. The alleged threat to the US by the Backfire has been used extensively by US arms planners to justify new expenditure on US air defences, although most experts agree that even were a Backfire to reach CONUS, it would be on a suicide mission, with no hope of useful retreat. The USN, in turn, has cited the Backfire's AS-4 Kitchen anti-ship missiles as justification for the development of its own expensive F-14 planes with their Phoenix missiles, although both systems predate Backfire.

See also **Badger, Blinder**

Badger the Russian Tupolev TU-16 twin-jet subsonic medium bomber. The Badger was the mainstay of the Soviet bombing forces in the 1960s and 1970s but is now being phased out of its bombing role. Only 440 planes of an original 2,000+ strong fleet remain in service. The Badger can deliver a 9-ton payload over short ranges, with a maximum range of 4,000 miles. It carries AS-5 (Kelt) and AS-6 (Kingfish) **SRAM** missiles.

balance of terror the current international stalemate which is based on the ability of both superpowers to wreak nuclear havoc on the other. Probably coined by Canadian PM Lester Pearson in 1955, on the tenth anniversary of the UN Charter, in saying 'The balance of terror has replaced the balance of power.'

See also **assured destruction, MAD**

BAMBI acronym for Ballistic Missile Boost Intercept. A scheme debated in the late 1960s which intended to use a low-orbit satellite to launch interceptors on warning of a missile attack; the interceptors would destroy the missiles while they were still in the first or boost phase of their flight. The plan was abandoned when it was apparent that the number of satellites required would be far too great. While BAMBI theories were replaced by other concepts of **ABM**, as recently as 1982 the scheme emerged again when the Heritage Foundation proposed a space-based ABM system which would consist of 450 orbiting battle stations armed with a total of 18,000–20,000 small interceptors. Each interceptor, weighing 100 lb, would use the non-nuclear Homing Intercept Technology (**HIT**) warhead, which was then still at the research stage of development. The scheme has not proceeded beyond the conceptual stage. In its desire to create a laser-activated defence umbrella over the West and shoot down any hostile missiles, President Reagan's Strategic Defence Initiative (**SDI**) may be seen as the current version of BAMBI.

See also **ABM, BMD, boost phase defence, SBL, SDI**

baroque armaments 'The offspring of a marriage between private enterprise and the state, between the capitalist dynamic of the arms manufacturers and the conservatism that tends to characterise armed forces . . . in peacetime' (Mary Kaldor, *The Baroque Arsenal*, 1982). The concept behind the 'baroque' view of arms manufacture is that the technology advances, but only within the limits of far less forward-looking theories of warfare – the perfection either of current trends, whereby hardware becomes increasingly complex and sophisticated, but actually delivers much the same end-product to the user as the original version, rather than any attempt at genuine revolutionary development, of weapons that would be cheaper to produce and equally effective in their use. As long as the military–industrial complex can see the power and the profits to be obtained from perpetuating the *status quo*, this situation is bound to continue. The phrase was coined by US nuclear physicist Herbert York, who spoke of 'baroque, even rococo varieties of A bombs and H bombs' in *The Race to Oblivion* (1970).

basic encyclopedia the compilation for military use of all local military installations and points of similar importance to be known and considered in the event of an attack.

bear

(1) the Soviet Union.

(2) NATO term for any variety of Soviet bomber, each of which is given a name beginning with B (**Backfire**, **Badger**, **Bison**, **Blackjack**, **Blinder**); Soviet fighters are named with F prefixes (**Fagot**, **Fishbed**, **Flagon**, **Flogger**, **Foxbat**, etc.).

Bear Russian Tupolev TU-95 long-range strategic bomber,

introduced in 1955. It flies at 550 mph, delivering an 11-ton bomb load over a range of 8,000 miles. The latest version, the Bear-F, is used for anti-submarine warfare. As a strategic weapons platform the Bear suffers from its very large radar signature, intensified by its four turboprop blades.

See also **Bison**

B

benign testing the testing of a new weapons system in such a way that it will perform as the makers, and the military who commissioned it, desire. Such excellent performance is significantly aided by a variety of underhand means or simple lies, such as the excellent results ascribed to the AMRAAM, a new US air-to-air missile tested in 1982. Such results were helped by the sound-emitting device placed in the target drone, tuned to attract the incoming missile. When this stratagem was discovered, USAF explained that they had not wished 'to bore anyone with technical details'.

bent spear the US emergency code to denote an incident (less potentially dangerous than an accident) involving a nuclear device. Thus it ranks below any accident, as well as any possibility of 'war risk detonation'.

bids and proposals 'The expenses incurred by defense contractors or would-be contractors in response to official requests for proposals concerning weapons and weapons technology . . .'. Such expenses are used as a convenient cover-all to hide additional defence expenditure over and above the regular sums sanctioned by Congress.

Big Bird the best-known of the US system of surveillance/'spy' satellites, the first of the fleet being put into orbit in June 1971. One of these 12-ton satellites is in the sky at a time, flying a low polar orbit for four or five months. Big Bird has area surveillance, close-look visible light cameras, infra-red and multi-spectral sensors, side-looking radar and a TV camera equipped with a zoom lens. The satellite is capable of manoeuvring through clouds to take a closer look at a specified area. It transmits information to a variety of ground stations across the world, each of which relays the information to the satellite control facility in Sunnyvale, Calif. Capsules of film ejected from Big Bird are scooped out of the air as they fall, by a special aircraft based in Hawaii.

Big Blue Cube the Satellite Test Center, the command headquarters of the USAF Space Division's Satellite Control Facility. A nine-storey, windowless, pale-blue block, with administrative buildings and radar and communications installations attached. Sited in Sunnyvale, California, the STC is conveniently near Lockheed, whose employees, who run the mission control centres, outnumber the air force personnel. From the STC are controlled the seven Satellite Control Facility stations based around the world which together control forty-five US military satellites, making some 90,000 annual contacts with the orbiting fleet. Plans at STC include the improvement of electronic contact with the satellites, and the phasing out of the seven remote facilities, possibly with an extra satellite – the Satellite Control Satellite – which would monitor those in space before sending information back to one ground station in the US.

big one US strategic intelligence code for a Soviet missile test.

bin to discard a weapons system from the current inventories after it has been tried in battle and determined to be inadequate.

binary weapon a shell or bomb filled with two chemicals that remain harmless while kept separate but which mix on impact to provide a fatally toxic substance for use in chemical/biological warfare. Those nerve gases reprocessed for binary use include Binary Sarin and Binary VX. Launchers for binary weapons include two types of projectile for use with the US 155 mm howitzer, one for the 8-inch howitzer, and 500 lb spray-bombs for the F-4 and F-111 aircraft.

See also **CW**

Bison the Russian MY Asischev M-4 subsonic four-jet long-range strategic bomber, introduced in 1956; the approximate equivalent to the US B-52. Generally inferior to the B-52, the Bison carries only 25 per cent of the US plane's payload, is not equipped with stand-off missiles, and has a lower ceiling than the B-52. It was the introduction of the Bison at the Tushino

Air Show, when a US diplomat noted what appeared to be a large number of the planes circling above the airfield, that created the 'bomber gap' fantasies of the 1950s. In fact, the Bison fleet was still small, but for effect the same group of bombers flew backwards and forwards over the airfield. As the CIA quickly revised upwards their estimates of USSR bomber strength, the effect might be said to have worked satisfactorily.

See also **Bear**

black boxes modular components that can easily be moved or replaced as necessary in the event of a parts failure in the case of a particular weapon or aircraft. Black boxes are behind much of modern military design which aims for ease of maintenance, but the potential uses of such schemes are often laid low by a lack of available parts, including the boxes themselves.

Blackjack the Soviet RAM-P (TU-X) variable geometry (swing-wing) supersonic penetration/stand-off bomber, tested in the mid-1980s for possible production and deployment in the 1990s. Although information on the Blackjack is limited, the plane is expected to be somewhat larger than the US **B1-B**, flying at Mach 2.3 to deliver a payload of at least 16 tons (much less than the B1-B's scheduled 28 tons) over a range of more than 8,000 miles.

See also **Backfire**

Blinder the Russian Tupolev TU-22 supersonic medium-range twin-jet bomber. Russia's first supersonic bomber was deployed in 1962. Despite problems as to range, 165 Blinders were in service in 1985, flying up to 1,300 miles (extendable with aerial refuelling) in two versions. The TU-22A carries gravity nuclear bombs; the TU-22B carries a single A-4 stand-off missile mounted externally.

See also **Badger, Backfire**

blowtorch USAF slang for a jet fighter, referring to the after-burners which flame on take-off.

blue force in the military exercises and war 'games' performed by NATO forces, blue signifies friendly forces.

See also **orange force**

blue on blue contact the meeting, in the air, of one friendly patrol with another.
See also **blue force**

blue suits the military personnel on an airbase, as opposed to a civilian contractor's employees who often work on the hardware – planes and control systems – which have been manufactured by their firm. Thus at the USAF Satellite Test Centre 885 air force employees work alongside 926 people employed by Lockheed.
See also **white suits**

blue water navy naval forces committed to operating in the blue water, i.e. the open sea. Used thus since nineteenth century.
See also **brown water navy**

blunting mission retaliatory action, presumably employing nuclear weapons, designed to destroy enemy *materiel.*
See also **counterforce strike**

BMD acronym for ballistic missile defence. Specifically designed as one of the possible ways of protecting the **MX** missile, but to be deployed against attacks on any US ICBM silos. The drawback to BMD is that under the still-extant **ABM** Treaty of 1972, such 'anti-missile missiles' are banned by the superpowers. Nonetheless research – split into the Advanced Technology Program and the Systems Technology Program (which turns basic research into usable hardware and guidance systems) – continues. The intention of current BMD research is to create a 'layered defence', destroying the bulk of missiles during either the boost or mid-course phase of the missile's flight, and attempting to mop up the remainder in the terminal phase, in which the missile re-enters the atmosphere above its target. The layers in question are the exo-atmospheric layer (above 300,000 feet) and the lower endo-atmospheric layer. A major concept is **LoAD** (Low Altitude Defence) which would be based on a system designed to intercept ICBM re-entry vehicles, discriminating real from decoy warheads and from jettisoned ICBM tanks. A further theory would use LoAD as a final line of defence, with some form of non-nuclear means positioned outside the atmosphere which would thin out the incoming missiles before they began re-entry. The **SDI**, the so-called 'Star Wars' project, is the ultimate projection of such theories of defence in what the eponymous pressure group who most fervently support the initiative call 'the High Frontier'.

See also **ABM, boost phase defence, SDI**

BMEWS acronym for Ballistic Missile Early Warning System.

See also **NORAD**

boob acronym for bolt out of the blue. A surprise mission for USAF pilots; descended from the RAF World War Two 'scramble'.

boomers USN nickname for strategic submarines (**SSBN**s) such as Poseidons and Trident Is.

See also **strategic submarines**

boost phase defence defences against incoming missiles which concentrate on destroying them during the first, boost phase (or powered flight phase) of their flight, at which time the booster engines are emitting a brilliant flame and the multiple warheads have not yet been launched. Given the long distances at which such operations must be carried out, such defence is generally ascribed to laser weaponry which will be guided onto its targets by sensors responsive to the infra-red emissions of the rocket engines.

See also **BMD, SBL, SDI**

boy any nuclear device that explodes successfully.

breakout the ability of one superpower to escape from the limitations of the threat currently posed by the capability of the other. As seen by pessimistic US officials, this is the theory that the Soviets are continually searching for loopholes in arms control treaties; they will exploit such loopholes by preparing a sudden unexpected surge in military force – constructing such weapons as have not been banned, or which are capable of ambiguous interpretation as to their permitted deployment – and thus creating a dramatic and anti-US shift in the balance of power. To this end the problems of verification are magnified, as are the problems of the fine points of treaties, especially the categorising of missiles – what, for instance, might stop the Soviets deploying missiles with conventional warheads, storing an equivalent number of nuclear warheads conveniently nearby and then swapping them if a crisis was moving towards war? The fear of breakout is endemic to the arms race and to the apparent inability of arms talks to reach positive conclusions.

brick RN use; any projectile – rocket, missile, shell, etc.
See also **rock**

brinkmanship from the declaration in 1956 by US Secretary of State, John Foster Dulles, 'if you are scared to go to the brink, you are lost. . . . We walked to the brink and we looked it in the face.' A method of conducting international relations (especially between the US and the Soviets) on a level only marginally short of declared war. The Cuban Missile Crisis of 1961 was probably the supreme instance of the art since the word was coined.

broken arrow the US Department of Defense Nuclear Accident Code, divided into five degrees of severity: (1) unauthorised or accidental detonation; no risk of war; (2) non-nuclear detonation of a nuclear device; (3) radioactive contamination; (4) seizure, theft or loss (including emergency jettisoning) of the weapon; (5) any public hazard contingent upon nuclear weapons, actual or implied.

broken-backed war
(1) (nuclear) such fighting as might continue assuming that **first** and **second strikes** and **retaliation** had all failed to settle the conflict and that any survivors either wished to or had the capability of fighting on. Such a war must be the logical conclusion of current US concepts of **survivability** and 'winnable' nuclear exchanges.
(2) (conventional) the continuing resistance by a guerilla force after the main army of their side has been otherwise defeated.

brown water navy naval forces that patrol the coastal areas of a nation's sea defence system.

brushfire operations skirmishes; improvised short-lived conflicts conducted on a limited scale, often by or against guerillas.

B

brushfire wars small wars which, like brushfires, flare up and then die down again quickly. They do not involve the superpowers directly – although the armaments on which they depend will almost certainly have originated with one or other of them or their major allies – but like brushfires they can spread and grow out of control.
See also **austere wars, brushfire operations**

bud an **ICBM**.
See also **brick, rock**

build-down the concept that for every new weapon added to a superpower's arsenal, a number of old weapons must be put into retirement. The policy was formulated in May 1983 by three US senators, tired of the impasse in the **START** talks and wishing to develop a plan that, unlike those preferred by the advocates of the **Midgetman** missile or of de-**MIRV**ing current missiles, maintained US arms production on schedule. The plan was initially popular – not only did it provide a possible means of moving START along, but its support for the **MX** programme in particular endeared it to many senators who worried that the public would turn against arms development if the Administration seemed powerless to advance arms control. The Administration's experts disliked the plan, particularly for its willingness to rationalise the asymmetry between the two opposing **strategic triads** and to accept that any reductions must involve tradeoffs of US bombers for Soviet missiles. By October 1983, as the START stalemate persisted, the whole of Congress united – the build-downers in the Senate and the de-MIRVers and Midgetman supporters in the House of Representatives. A scheme was developed which incorporated the warhead ceilings of the President's Eureka speech (see **START**), the development of Midgetman and the concomitant de-MIRVing, and the overall reductions specified by the build-downers. Faced by this unity, the Administration set out to create its own version of the plan which could them be incorporated in the US side of START. The result was a development of build-down – double build-down. This scheme was based on two novel concepts, the 'potential destructive capacity' and the 'standard weapon stations' possessed by each of the superpowers; in other words, the total ballistic missile **throw-weight** and the number of individual warheads – the lowest common denominator of 'strategic attack capability' – held by each side. The latter were to be assessed on a flexible scale: MIRVs counted higher, as did the Soviet 'heavy' SS-18s; bombers were to be counted as to the armaments they carried. The basis of double build-down was that each side would have to reduce by certain set percentages over time both the number of individual warheads and the number of standard weapon stations.

This plan, with its 'something for everyone' philosophy, seemed to satisfy its US clients, but made no impression on the Russians – for all that they were included in the 'everyone', with the suggestion that both sides would be cutting back to the same extent. The experts in Washington were not surprised. So complex and novel was double build-down that it would be hard enough to explain it to the US public; the Russians were never really expected to embrace a plan that was so different to the arms talks *status quo*. In the event double build-down ended START. The Soviets rejected what they called 'old poison in new bottles', and rejected suggestions that they study the plan as 'a worthless exercise'. On 8 December, a fortnight after the Soviets had walked out of the **INF talks**, their compatriots at START did just the same.

See also **START**

bus the final stage of a nuclear **MIRV** missile, containing the guidance systems and directional jets as well as the nuclear warhead itself.

button on any form of military equipment or armament that can be fitted onto a vehicle subsequent to the basic version being issued to the troops, e.g. a machine gun that fits onto a helicopter, etc.

buy in an arms trade contractor 'buys in' to a contract by deliberately making a bid that he knows to be unrealistically low. Once this bid has been made and accepted it is rarely difficult to persuade the Pentagon to reassess the costs onto a

B

realistic, or even grossly inflated, level. Thus it is feasible for a firm to obtain a contract with a bid of, say, $1.9bn and, with no demur from the Pentagon, have the final costs reassessed at double that sum. It is also becoming clear that – as in the case of General Dynamics, the largest US arms manufacturer – the Pentagon accountants happily pass spurious 'expenses' claims without a query. General Dynamics has been heavily fined for its excesses – such as charging the cost of a new mattress when the one supplied to an executive in a hotel was not to his liking – but the real wastage, on whole weapons systems that are required only to create jobs and profits, remains on the whole unregulated.

See also **baroque armaments**

C

C

C ring a circular area centred on **ground zero** in which the **overpressure** is measured at 1.5–6 psi. In this area blast could cause lethal flying missiles, such as shards of shattered glass.
See also **A ring, B ring**

C³CM acronym for control, command and communications counter-measures. Aspects of electronic warfare which aim to discover hostile C3 and take electronic counter-measures – jamming, etc. – and then plan a systematised method of attack and destruction. In the ideal development, friendly C3 should be able to defend itself from attack by its superior technology.
See also **C³I**

C³I acronym for control, command and communications intelligence. In essence the ability of commanders to manipulate their forces in battle, 'c-cubed' or 'C³' has, alongside '**Star Wars**', become the central factor of US nuclear strategy today. The need for a commander to know what is going on and to order his battle accordingly is as old as warfare; the increasing sophistication of military communications has only added technology to this basic requirement. C³I falls into three areas – early warning sensors, command posts and communications; all three are interdependent, but without the third, the other two are useless. Military communications, which take in conventional telephone lines, microwaves leased from commercial companies and dedicated military links (including an increasing number of satellites and their earth terminals) are vital but vulnerable. Apart from simple jamming and bombing, all such links suffer the threat of electro-magnetic pulse (**EMP**) – a direct product of nuclear explosions and one which will destroy even the most sophisticated technology. Satellites, which control two-thirds of

US military communications, are especially vulnerable to EMP. The current aim is to 'EMP-harden' any new satellite links. The contemporary obsession with C³I dates from President Carter's **PD** (Presidential Directive) **59** (1980) in which the US was required to consider ways of fighting a prolonged nuclear war, reversing the ruling concept of **assured destruction** and replacing it with that of **survivability**, **endurance** and winnable nuclear wars. Based itself on PD 53 (which first considered nuclear war as a series of prolonged retaliatory strikes) and PD 58, which dealt with the continuity of government during and after a nuclear exchange, PD-59 was embraced by President Reagan; his National Security Directive 12 (1981) underlined the new belief that a nuclear war could be won. In the Reagan plan, the whole spectrum of C³I will be reassessed and improved. A vast array of new technology, most particularly in satellite and laser communications, is scheduled for development, all tending towards the basic theory that the best way of preventing a war is to show the USSR that US intelligence, let alone fire power, is so strong that no effort they make can be worthwhile. In effect, C³I is seen as the ideal means of escalation control. While the **MX** missile and 'Star Wars' find Congressional opposition, C³I is regularly voted increasing amounts, totalling 10 per cent of the US defence budget. Foremost amongst the plans is the development of **MILSTAR**, a communications satellite resistant to jamming and EMP, destined to link all US nuclear forces. Yet all these sophisticated communications, linked to **WWMCCS** (the US Worldwide Military Command and Control System) are by no means foolproof. On the one hand, such intensity of intelligence may even swamp the commanders for whom it is prepared. More disturbingly, a 1982 report made it clear that all this hi-tech material cannot be guaranteed to work, even under optimum conditions; under a nuclear attack, every new installation becomes simply one more vulnerable target. And, perhaps most importantly, the increasing devolution of responsibility from human to electronic intelligence, with all its fallibility, makes ever more likely the chance of an unstoppable 'accident' that leads irrevocably into nuclear war.

See also **C³CM, kneecap, MEECN, NMCC, NMCS, WWMCCS**

C⁴I acronym for command, control, communication, computation and identification.
See also **C³I**

cab-rank patrol a technique of close air support. Instead of taking off and flying straight to a predestined target which should then be destroyed and abandoned, the planes loiter in the air, waiting for targets of opportunity, the existence of which is revealed to them by ground control.

CAESAR the linked-array underwater sonar systems, positioned around the US continental shelf, that warn against surprise penetration by Soviet **SSBN**s.
See also **ABM**

capability
(1) war plans.
(2) the possession of a range of weaponry by a nation or a military force. Overall capability is usually defined further, e.g. **first strike**, **look-down shoot-down**, **multiple kill**, **second strike**, **termination**, etc.
See also **credibility**

CAPTOR acronym for Encapsulated Torpedoes. A deep-water anti-submarine 'smart' mine consisting of a Mark-46 torpedo fitted into an 11-foot-long mine casing with acoustic sensors and a miniature computer. CAPTOR is anchored on the ocean floor at depths of up to 2,500 feet to listen to shipping and submarine traffic. When it hears the signature of a hostile submarine, the mine is released and a code buoy is floated to the surface where it sends a cryptic message reporting time of release and number of the mine. The intention of CAPTOR is to bottle up the Soviet submarine fleet; it is estimated that if just 500 mines are 'seeded' in the narrow passages that the Soviet navy must pass through to gain open water away from its ports, this object can be achieved. A second version of the mine is being developed for shallower waters, notably the continental shelves.
See also **ASW**

carpet an electronic device used to jam radar reception.

catalytic war a war between two nations which is brought about by the actions of a third which precipitates hostilities by acting as a catalyst for their hitherto restrained animosity.
See also **austere wars**

C

CBMs acronym for confidence building measures. Mutually agreed measures designed to eliminate the inevitable distrust endemic to arms limitations agreements between the superpowers. CBMs aim to help verify that agreements are actually maintained by either side. Methods of achieving this include the establishment of committees, e.g. the Standing Consultative Commission (established in 1972 under **SALT I** and renewed by **SALT II** in 1979), and mutually supplied inventories of those weapons held by each side and covered by a given agreement. Above all the intention is to cut down the possibilities of a war started not by intent but by misunderstanding. The problem with CBMs is that they have little validity in a vacuum, and that they are often used as a substitute for more substantial and tangible agreements. As one US official at the START talks put it, 'they're just frosting on the cake'. The final problem, epitomised by President Reagan's sabre-rattling speeches or the Soviet's colonial ambitions in the Third World, is what use are such positive words when general policy seems so opposed to them?

cemetery network in NATO code the main nuclear forces command radio links, based on a high frequency (HF) radio network.

CEP acronym for circular error probable. The radius of a circle in which it is computed that half of all missiles delivered by any given weapons system are expected to land. The lower the CEP, the more accurate the system; modern missiles can assume an accuracy of a few metres. With the development of manoeuvrable re-entry vehicles (**MARV**) and the future deployment of the **NAVSTAR** global positioning system, the guidance and thus accuracy of missiles has developed substantially, and with it the decreasing width of the CEP. It is this new accuracy that lies behind the drive towards mobile launching systems, notably the intermediate range Soviet SS-20 and US **cruise** varieties and the intercontinental SS-X-24 and **MX**, both of which are apparently capable of 'killing' a hardened target. Yet there remain limitations to this vaunted accuracy, stemming not from the military hardware, but from the anomalies in nature itself. Conditions are not always stable or even predictable; the earth is not a perfect sphere and thus its gravitational pull varies as to area. Such gravitational differences are by no means accurately mapped, yet they can make substantial differences in missile accuracy. An inertial guidance system, as used on missiles, is not infallible – it cannot differentiate between the vehicle's movement and the effects of gravity. Thus it may make unnecessary compensation for the latter, sending the missile off course. Missile experts are trying, and have a good chance of succeeding, to map the differences in the earth's gravity, which in turn can be fed into targeting and guidance computers. They have less chance of predicting the weather for the target area on the day that war breaks out. Wind speed can force missiles off course; a 30 mph wind can cause a 1,320-foot drift outside its computed lethal radius on the target. Efforts to correct this problem have their own inbuilt difficulties. Fast-fliers can defeat wind speed, but their own improved velocity can make them vulnerable to other weather conditions, e.g. severe storms, in which simple raindrops can become hard-hitting projectiles as the combined speeds add together. Certainly the endlessly evolving technology means that more and more of these anomalies can be overcome, but the uncertainties do remain. In the end, all the theories can have only one solution – the actualities of use in war. And at that stage it will be too late to adjust the missiles further.

chaff strips of metal foil released to jam radar scanners and/or the guidance systems of missiles, especially in air combat. The system was developed by the UK and Germany in World War II.

See also **window**

cheeseburger (*or* big blue eighty-two, daisycutter) the BLU/82/B11 concussion bomb, 11 feet long, 4.5 feet wide, weighing 7.5 tons and containing over 6 tons of gelled aqueous slurry of ammonium nitrate, polystyrene soap and aluminium powder. Only a nuclear weapon is more powerful than this bomb, which sends a mushroom cloud 6,000 feet into the air and, if exploded 3 feet above the ground, creates a blast **over-pressure** of 1,000 psi which will kill everything (including the worms beneath the surface) in a surrounding area of 755 acres, and most things within 2,000 acres.

C

Chevaline the development during the 1970s and 1980s of a new 'front-end' for the ageing Polaris A-3 missiles with which the UK strategic submarines are armed (until the **Trident** programme replaces them from 1992). The name 'Chevaline' allegedly stems from the US 'Antelope-1' programme, designed to create an **SLBM** that concentrated on penetrating **ABM** defences rather than on **MIRV**ed accuracy. The 'Chevaline', according to the UK Ministry of Defence, is a species of antelope, more a mountain goat, that, like the 'front-end' named for it, can manoeuvre at high altitudes. The update is intended to counter anti-missile defences, notably the **Galosh** system surrounding Moscow, and combines new warheads with a variety of penetration aids and decoys. This interim programme, which has cost *c.* £1bn (1980 prices) has suffered a number of technical holdups and was not deployed until 1982, with completion on all four UK **SSBN**s expected by 1988. Chevaline was initially reported to have armed each missile with six multiple re-entry vehicles (**MRV**) of 50 KT each, but more recent accounts (there are no official figures) suggest a 2xMRV or MIRV system, which confirms Ministry of Defence assurances that Chevaline will not increase UK warhead numbers.

See also **Moscow criterion, SLBM**

chicken button (*or* chicken switch)
(1) a switch or button operated from the launch site that can destroy a malfunctioning rocket or missile in midflight.
(2) a switch or button that an astronaut or jet pilot can use to eject his capsule from a malfunctioning rocket, or his seat from a potentially crashing plane.

chicks friendly fighter aircraft.

chop acronym for change of operational control.

christmas tree
(1) an indicator panel on a submarine which flashes red and green lights to show whether hatches, valves, etc., are locked tight when the submarine dives.
(2) a combat uniform belt worn by an infantryman and adorned with grenades, knife, flask, flares and whatever else is required for a battle or assault.

chuffing the characteristic of some rocket engines to burn intermittently and with odd, irregular noises, reminiscent of an 'old banger' on the London to Brighton vintage car run.
See also **chugging**

chugging low frequency oscillations. The irregular explosions of exhaust gases from a rocket motor. To move with the sound of an electric or steam engine.
See also **chuffing**

chumming a night air attack strategy involving two planes. One keeps its lights on and thus draws fire from the target; this naturally pinpoints the target and leaves it vulnerable to attack from the second plane, which has kept its lights off.

city-busting (*or* counter-city) the targeting and presumed 'busting' of urban centres in a nuclear war. Such attacks on 'soft' targets are central to the **MAD** doctrine and the concept of the '**balance of terror**'; city-busting missiles would be set to explode above the target in an airburst, thus creating maximum damage and radioactive fallout.
See also **countervalue**

clandestine cache secret supplies of fissionable material held within the borders of a nation that is ostensibly party to a disarmament treaty. Such caches offer the potential of making nuclear weapons and may well have been hived off from supplies openly obtained for use in nuclear fuel reactors.

classical figure that amount of special material that provides a critical mass for the manufacturing of nuclear bombs – 20 kilograms of enriched uranium.

clean
(1) a nuclear device that produces maximum blast and thermal effects, but keeps radiation fallout to a minimum, thus, theoretically, producing most of the resultant deaths as an immediate result of the explosion itself rather than from the radiation sickness that will develop among its victims over the succeeding months.
(2) an aircraft that carries no external stores, e.g. extra fuel tanks, extra weapons, etc., above its usual complement.
(3) an aircraft with its landing gear retracted.
See also **air burst**

cold launch (*or* pop-up) the system used to launch a missile without igniting its fuel in the silo. Low pressure gas is used to push the rocket upwards; the engine is then ignited in the air after it has cleared the launch site, and leaves the silo unharmed, ready for further use. The cold launch technique is to be used, *inter alia*, on the **MX** 'Peacekeeper' missile.

collateral damage civilian casualties that are the inevitable by-product of a nuclear attack and of virtually any battlefield.

comint abbreviation for communications intelligence. The monitoring, by a network of listening stations sited around the borders of the USSR, of government and military communications; US linguistics specialists man these posts to record and, when useful, transcribe Soviet radio traffic for use in the overall US intelligence picture. Such interceptions are usually of '*en clair*' or low-level code messages. Created in the 1950s to service the USAF's need for maximum intelligence for the targeting of Soviet airfields, garrisons, etc., comint has declined in the face of increasing dependence on satellite communications. As the listening posts are reduced – either through budgetary cutbacks or, as in the case of Iran, the ascendancy of an anti-US government – more and more comint, in its original man-manipulated form, has been abandoned and replaced by electronic monitors, at which point it has become **elint**.
See also **elint, humint, sigint, telint**

conflict spectrum all levels of hostility in a nuclear war, from

the first pre-crisis wrangling and sabre-rattling, through a graduated escalation to **first-** and **second-strike** nuclear exchanges.
See also **escalation**

connectivity the ensuring by nuclear war planners that when a war actually begins, all plans, personnel and *materiel* involved will link up and work as required and intended.
See also **strategic connectivity**

C

controlled counterforce war a nuclear war in which military concentration is on reducing enemy strategic retaliatory forces and the intention is to minimise civilian casualties.
See also **city-busting, counterforce**

CONUS acronym for the continental United States.

conventional forces, war, weapons
(1) armaments that have been sanctioned by agreement or prior usage and which conform to standard international agreements on their acceptability.
(2) military organisations, hostilities and hardware that do not have or use a nuclear capability.

corridor bashing the saturation bombing of hostile airfields, lines of communication and vital facilities.

counterforce a nuclear strike against the enemy's military forces and weapons rather than at his cities and civilians; thus counterforce weapons, counterforce option, counterforce strike, etc. Developed during the era of unassailable US nuclear ascendancy in the 1950s, counterforce gave way for ten years to **MAD**, with its threat to civilian as well as military areas, but since Secretary of Defense Schlesinger's NSDM-242 of 1974 (providing for more flexible inter-power tactics, even after the first and retaliatory strikes) the concept of hitting only military targets has gained increasing strength; the signing of **PD-59** confirmed the belief that, far from '**assured destruction**', there can exist 'winnable' nuclear wars – fought on a conventional, if intercontinental, battlefield with unconventional weapons – which, like any other engagement, can and will be fought to a finish. While improved accuracy and a shrinking **CEP** do make such surgical targeting feasible, the hardening of missile silos at 2,500 psi (a brick house explodes at 5–10 psi) means that their destruction will require more than a single warhead. This renders all calculations dubious since multiple explosions are subject to **fratricide** – the yet-to-be-tested assumption that the force of the first explosion will inevitably undermine the performance of subsequent missiles. Likewise, military installations are by no means restricted to areas conveniently isolated from civilian centres. Thus, while counterforce suits prevailing theories, and represents to some a massive temptation to use the nuclear arsenal, it is unlikely that the supposed 'limited war' that such targeting promises could be in the event anything more than a pious, if useful, theory.

See also **countervalue**

countervailing strategy the war-fighting strategy initiated by Secretary of Defense James Schlesinger in 1974 and encapsulated in President Carter's **PD-59** (1980). The strategy would assure that no potential adversary of the US or its allies would ever conclude that aggression would be worth the costs that would be incurred, on whatever level of conflict contemplated. In many ways this resembled the **massive retaliation** of the 1950s, but now there could be no assumption of US superiority, only the promised development of such new weapons and **C³I** that would ensure that the US threat held due substance. Although Carter attempted to set this strategy up as something quite new, it was no more than part, as his Secretary of Defense Harold Brown stressed, of the continually evolving US nuclear policy; indeed, for all that the Reagan administration likes to set itself against the 'weak' Carter years, the US position in the mid-1980s can be traced directly back to the countervailing strategy.

See also **PD-59**

countervalue the targeting of enemy cities and other resources that constitute the social fabric of a state. This strategy, with its concomitant '**balance of terror**' holding the world's populations to ransom, forms the basis of the **assured destruction** which dominated superpower nuclear strategies during the 1960s and which, despite the development of **counterforce** and **Star Wars** theories, threatens millions of people today. While counterforce targeting might well intend to avoid civilian centres, the inextricability of military installations and the human population around them renders such promises all too optimistic.

See also **collateral damage, counterforce, MAD**

coupling usually known as strategic coupling. The policy that links an ostensibly low-level conflict, e.g. any signs of Soviet or Warsaw Pact aggression in Europe, to the immediate justification for a US use of strategic nuclear weapons. NATO planning has consistently made it clear to the Russians that any attack on Europe will trigger a response from the US; the Soviets, on the other hand, persist in attempting to 'decouple' Europe and the US by capitalising on European anti-war movements, offering deals that would benefit European leaders, playing on European fears that the US would fight World War III in European territory, etc.

Cover All a converted Boeing 707 with a crew of twenty-one which acts as the Strategic Air Command's airborne command post. Cover All planes patrol in three eight-hour shifts twenty-four hours a day, flying at 30,000 feet above the US on constant alert. On board the plane is a Brigadier-General, the lowest rank with authorised access to the nuclear **go codes**. Despite the constant patrolling of Cover All planes, and the intentions to 'harden' them against a nuclear attack, it is in fact accepted that the planes would be unlikely to survive, or be of real use, after a **first strike** attack.

See also **Looking Glass, Nightwatch**

cratology the 'science' of obtaining intelligence data by analysing the crates, boxes, containers and similar anonymous packages carried by a target boat, plane, train or truck. Given that these crates tend to be sealed, such information is necessarily highly speculative and must be confirmed by further, more accurate, sources.

See also **dentology**

credibility the concept of ensuring that an enemy believes that you mean what you say and will do what you threaten; also the ability to reassure an ally that you will do what you have promised. Thus **credible deterrent** – a weapons system (*de facto* nuclear) which you have convinced the enemy that you are ready and willing to use and which will prove itself as destructive as billed.

See also **capability**

C

Creek Misty airborne reconnaissance flights carried out by NATO forces over Europe.

crisis management a synonym for inter-superpower relations, coined by US Secretary of Defense Robert MacNamara after the Cuban Missile Crisis of 1961 – 'There is no longer any such thing as strategy, only crisis management.' The concept that foreign relations have become, in essence, a process of keeping such international crises that do occur beneath such a level that might escalate irrevocably into conflict.

crit abbreviation for critical mass. The minimum mass or size of fissile material required to set off a chain reaction in a nuclear weapon.

See also **fission, fusion**

cross-targeting the practice of targeting two warheads from different missiles on the same target, particularly used to guarantee the destruction of a hardened target. Cross-targeting is always restricted to one pair of missiles since the problems of **fratricide** would probably negate the accuracy of any further warheads. Cross-targeting assumes that both missiles will arrive on target as desired.

cruise missiles the cruise missile is essentially a small, pilotless airplane that hugs the ground and uses its on-board radar and guidance system to deliver a nuclear (or conventional) warhead over great distances and with sufficient accuracy to threaten hard targets. The air launched cruise missile (**ALCM**); ground launched cruise missile (**GLCM**) and sea launched cruise missile (**SLCM**) (respectively pronounced 'alkum', 'glickem' and 'slickem') which make up the 'family' of cruise missiles are all based on what is ostensibly the ideal contemporary weapon – cheap to produce, carrying a substantial nuclear (or conventional) payload, flexible in its launch sites and equipped with sophisticated terrain-mapping technology (**TERCOM**) that will permit it to elude hostile radar as it proceeds to deliver its warhead within mere yards of its target. The concept of a pilotless 'drone' weapon dates back to 1915 when Dr Elmer Sperry, inventor of the directional gyroscope, created an 'aerial torpedo' or 'automatic flying bomb' which achieved a successful flight of 1,000 yards in 1918. At the same time the Germans were experimenting with a drone which was to be launched from Zeppelins onto a suitable target. The Armistice and the moves to disarmament in the 1920s effectively halted such research, but Hitler's V-1 and V-2 rockets re-opened interest in such weapons. Both superpowers had a prototype 'cruise' (the American Mace, the Russian Shaddock) but their inadequacies only reinforced the military preference on both sides for static **ICBM**s. In 1970 the current generation of 'drones', today's cruise, entered full-scale development when the Nixon administration authorised a $40m budget for the development of the subsonic armed decoy (SCAD), initially an electronic counter-measure (**ECM**) for the B-1 bomber. The B-1 was scrapped in 1977 (although its successor, the **B1-B**, was revived in 1982) but cruise continued in development. It soon rivalled **Trident** and the **MX** as the US's most vital strategic weapon (albeit at intermediate rather than strategic range), but, for reasons quite extraneous to its capabilities, cruise has become a byword for the problems of the nuclear warriors.

The European Nuclear Planning Group (NPG) had originally welcomed this latest example of US technology. It soon proved too simple a choice. The mishandling of the **enhanced radiation weapon** (neutron bomb) issue, the subsequent resurgence of international anti-nuclear activism and the barely concealed policy of the Reagan administration that Europe could be sacrificed for America in a nuclear war, have all conspired to make cruise highly unpopular, especially in Europe where, given its short-range (maximum 2,000 km) delivery, it has to be based. If the protestors of Greenham Common have failed to stop a single cruise from being sited (the first squadron of sixteen missiles arrived there on 14 November 1983), they have certainly helped point up its unpopularity. On a wider scale, cruise (especially in its ground- and sea-launched versions) has become a political rather than simply a military weapon. At the **SALT II** and **START** talks, as the latest bargaining chip, it was played off against the Russian **Backfire** bomber and SS-22 missiles. 'Cruise puts a new chip on the table, and all newness is destabilising' C. Campbell (1982). Mr Reagan claims that cruise, a 'slow-flier', should not be balanced against the 'fast-flier' Russian SS missiles. The Russians are unimpressed with an argument that they see as demanding simply that American technology is all that will keep world peace and that the US should be allowed to use it as, when and where they choose.

Current cruise missile types are as follows. (1) Sea-launched: TASM tactical anti-ship missile Tomahawk BGM109/BE; TLAM-C conventional land attack missile Tomahawk BGM109C; TLAM-N nuclear land attack missile. A total of 900 of all these, with a range of 2,500 km, are to be deployed in submarines and destroyers by 1987. All SLCMs are to be fuelled with TH-Dimer and Shelldyne-H propellants for maximum efficiency. (2) Air launched: medium-range air-to-surface missile (MRASM), an air-to-ground high-priority-target conventional attack missile; ALCM air-to-ground missile with 2,500 km range, flying at 800 kph; plans for 170 Boeing B-52G bombers to be re-engineered and equipped to carry a payload of twenty ALCMs each by 1990. (3) Ground launched: Tomahawk BGM-109G, the land-based cruise missile now deployed in Europe; one combat flight comprises sixteen Tomahawk missiles on four transporter-launchers operated by two launch-control centres. One flight remains on quick reaction alert status at each base during normal state of readiness; during a full alert each flight is spread out to pre-arranged 'satellite stations'. Eighty per cent of GLCMs have nuclear warheads; the remainder carry conventional weapons, including airfield attack cluster munitions. (4) In 1984 a contract was awarded to Lockheed, specialists in anti-radar technology, for the development of a 'stealth' ALCM, the advanced cruise missile. This weapon will approach its target at higher than normal cruise altitude – thus making it more difficult for the Soviets to defend against all cruise threats – and will possess an autonomous all-weather guidance system using passive sensors to follow the terrain; this minimises the risk of detection associated with the TERCOM radar altimeter, used on other cruise missiles. An initial projection of 2,800 missiles is under development, carrying *c.* 200 KT over 3,000 miles and possibly using the **NAVSTAR** guidance system.

The Soviet response to these US missiles has been, apart from their diplomatic protests, to develop their own cruise programme. This is unlikely to equal US achievements in miniaturisation or in accuracy, but, like many Soviet weapons, the SS-20, the Soviet 'cruise', will be powerful and plentiful. Based on the top two stages of the defunct and unusable SS-16, the solid-fuelled SS-20 is deployed on a wheeled launch vehicle, of some mobility, although limited in cross country movement, nine of which constitute a brigade along with their support vehicles. The missile remains in the launch tube, to be elevated to the vertical by its vehicle prior to firing. This launcher should be capable of reloading. The SS-20 comes in three versions: a single 650 KT warhead delivered over 3,100 miles; 3×150 KT **MIRV** warheads over 3,100 miles; a single 50 KT warhead over 4,350 miles, which would make some parts of the US vulnerable if launched in eastern Siberia. Some 378 SS-20s have been deployed, with the final total probably reaching 400. A development of the SS-20, the SS-X-20 is supposedly under research, promising an advanced version of the current missile, possibly including a terminal guidance system like that of the Pershing 2, based on radar images of the target, making a final correction before impact. The Soviets also have the SS-CX-4, comparable to the US GLCM, for coast-to-ship short-range use.

crutches padded and reinforced supports that brace a bomb or missile to prevent any shifting or accidental release of the ordnance during flight or landing.

CSB acronym for closely spaced basing.
See also **dense pack**

CSCE acronym for Conference on Security and Cooperation in Europe. The so-called 'Helsinki Final Act' signed in August 1975 aimed to establish a variety of confidence building measures (**CBMs**) as well as provisions for aspects of security and disarmament. Those essentially agreed on: prior notification of the details and duration of any major troop manoeuvres; it was suggested that, 'in a spirit of reciprocity', states participating in this agreement would permit observers from other participant states; there should be a general movement towards the strengthening of European *détente* and the promotion of disarmament.

CW acronym for chemical warfare. Chemical weapons have existed since April 1915, when the Germans dispersed chlorine gas along a 4-mile front near Ypres. By 1918 some 100,000 tons of chemicals had been used by both sides, including phosgene and mustard gas. In 1925 a Geneva protocol outlawed the use of chemical weapons, with the proviso that they could still be used in self-defence and therefore there should be no ban on their 'defensive' development and stockpiling. After World War II, in which chemicals were reserved for the civilian population, these researches continued. Despite the USA's short-lived ban on such developments in 1969 and the signing by 109 countries (from both East and West) in 1972 of a UN Convention banning further stockpiling of biological weapons (toxins developed from natural rather than chemical substances) – and here, as usual, were carefully preserved the 'defensive use' loopholes – the current picture is one of accelerating interest in and development of CW. The US has some 42,000 tons of lethal material stockpiled, much of this admittedly obsolete, but steps are underway to remove that problem. Development today centres on **binary weapons** – two substances, harmless in themselves, but deadly once they are mixed; such chemicals can be packaged in shells and warheads, the deadly mixing occurring naturally on impact. Around 47,000 US troops specialise in chemicals. Less squeamish over CW, the Red Army's Military Chemical Troops – some 100,000 men – have long been acknowledged as dealing with the USSR's estimated 350,000 tons of chemical weapons. It is this 'chemical gap' (descendant of the bomber and missile gaps before it) that has been taken as a convenient justification for recent moves to 'legitimise' a once abhorrent weapon now being increasingly touted to the peoples of America and Europe. That the Soviets include tear gas, smoke and napalm as chemical weapons makes no difference to the perception of the 'gap'. While some countries – notably Norway and the Netherlands – refuse to maintain stockpiles on their territory and Germany and Italy remain forbidden the possession of such material, the UK, always a leading developer of 'defence' CW, has shifted its policy away from such cosmetic defence to an openly offensive posture.

Given the essentially short-range uses of CW, it is Europe that, like it or not, is slated to host this growing arsenal. CW can be delivered by many conventional weapons – rockets, mortars, missiles, artillery shells (the USA has some 3 million-plus 155 mm and 8 inch shells modified for binary nerve gases, and land-based cruise missiles can easily be equipped with CW warheads) – all of which are likely to be fired from European soil. CW offers one further appeal; holding an ambivalent position between nuclear and conventional weapons, it has provided a new bargaining chip for use amidst the complexities of super-power arms talks.

Current chemical weapons include: phosgene (coughing, retching, frothing, asphyxia – lethal); prussic acid (convulsions, asphyxia – lethal); nitrogen mustard (blisters, attacks skin tissue – possibly lethal); Sarin (developed by Germany in 1938, attacks nervous system, chronic respiratory problems – incapacitates); Tabun (developed by Germany in 1936, nerve agent causing blurred vision, muscular spasms – incapacitates); Soman (developed by Germany in 1944 to replace Sarin, breathing difficulties, nausea, muscular spasms, involuntary bowel movements – possibly lethal); VX (a 'persistent' version of Sarin, whose oil-like drops evaporate slowly and thus stay lethal for days); BZ (hallucinations, giddiness, slows down mental and physical reactions – incapacitates). BZ was dropped from US CW arsenals since it tended to make its victims act maniacally, rather than collapse conveniently. The main Russian nerve gas is VR-55, a version of Sarin.

See also **ABC warfare, integrated battlefield, NBC warfare**

D

D

dadcap acronym for dawn and dusk combat air patrol.

damage assessment the finding out as soon as possible just how much damage – offensive and defensive – has been caused in a nuclear exchange. The theorists of 'winnable' or 'protracted' nuclear wars base much of their planning on obtaining such assessments.
See also **AWDREY, damage limitation, IONDS**

damage limitation the concept, coined by Robert MacNamara in 1962 and beloved of strategists of 'winnable' nuclear wars, that judicious planning and targeting can limit the damage caused by exploding warheads, and thus the pervading effects of the conflict in a nuclear exchange. As far as US strategists are concerned, the damage that is to be 'limited' is that sustained by American cities; hostile targets must still be completely destroyed so as to minimise such damage at home. Thus the term, in reality, is simply a synonym for counterforce.
See also **counterforce, countervalue, damage assessment**

dark objects satellites which are functioning but which have never emitted regular, traceable electronic signals. Such satellites have been cited by theorists as prototype missile-carrying space weapons.
See also **dark satellites**

dark satellites special satellites used for military or intelligence purposes, incorporating special electronic counter-measures to reduce their 'visibility' to hostile sensors, radar, etc.
See also **dark objects**

DARPA acronym for Defense Advanced Research Projects Agency, sited at Kirtland Air Force Base, near Albuquerque,

New Mexico. The spearhead of US weapons development, currently dedicated to the development of satellites and laser weaponry, and satellite-borne early warning and intelligence sensors, and offering overall 'revolutionary new options for the future defense' of the US, thus 'pulling significantly ahead of . . . adversaries in capabilities for surveillance, target acquisition and homing guidance' (Robert Fossum, head of the agency, 1983).

See also **BMD, C³I, SBL, SDI**

Deaf-smack acronym for Defence Special Missile and Aeronautics Center. The monitoring centre at Fort Meade, Maryland, which operates surveillance and analysis of Soviet electronic intelligence, especially that relating to the telemetry of **ICBM** tests. Deaf-smack has also taken on many of the surveillance activities formerly allotted to **comint** listening posts.

See also **elint**

decapitation any attack which might be able to 'decapitate' the US nuclear war effort; that is, knock out the massively computerised US World-Wide Military Command and Control System (**WWMCCS**) which operates from thirty ultra-sophisticated centres around the world. If this concept proved true, then the military 'torso' would be rendered powerless once its 'head', containing the **C³I** facilities essential to warfighting, was lopped off. US estimates fear that no more than 100 Soviet missiles could achieve satisfactory destruction of command centres, vital government facilities and worldwide communications. It is in the hope of countering this threat that the current development in C³I is taking place.

decay the date of re-entry of a satellite into the earth's atmosphere, either through natural causes or on human/computer-activated command.

decoupling the decision by the US to sacrifice Europe, and the forces it holds there, rather than permit an international conflict to affect the US itself. Such a decision would fly in the face of the **coupling** theory, which presumes that the permitting of the US to base missiles in Europe will act as an extra guarantee against Russian incursions. Thus European leaders continue to encourage the deployment of missiles on their national soil. The logical extension of this European fear is that both superpowers might choose to fight a nuclear war outside their own boundaries, pitting NATO against the Warsaw Pact and preserving their own territory. It has also been perceived that US bases are not wholly deterrent in effect; if the Russians do launch an attack, the targets they will hit in Europe will doubtless be mostly American, but the populations who will suffer will be wholly indigenous. In the words of US Rear Admiral Gene LaRoque, 'There isn't any question, if there's a trade-off we'd rather trade the Russians London or Bonn than we would Washington or Boston. No there isn't any question. That's just the nature of international politics . . . We fought World War I in Europe, we fought World War II in Europe and if you dummies let us, we'll fight World War III in Europe.' Such bombast, for all that more diplomatic Americans ostensibly reject it, is picked up in Europe and in Russia, and the succession of Soviet suggestions for cut-backs, weapons freezes and so on are all seen by the US as attempting to exploit a possible breach in NATO and possibly to achieve the absolute decoupling of the alliance.

See also **coupling, FBS**

deep creep an attack on a hostile submarine by a friendly vessel while both craft are at maximum depth below the surface of the ocean.

deep engagement a ground forces strategy which involves attacking the enemy well beyond the **FEBA** (the contact zone of a head-to-head battle), thus relieving the pressure on one's own front-line troops and artillery. In essence, the traditional concept of hitting the enemy behind their lines to create confusion and to divert troops from the main battlefield.

deep-basing a concept of nuclear defence strategy whereby a team of tunnellers accompany military personnel into a deep, hardened shelter to wait out the initial exchanges in a nuclear war. Weeks, or possibly months, after these have subsided, the idea is for these tunnellers to drill their way back up to the surface, create a makeshift silo and launch those missiles that have been deliberately kept in reserve. Such a final strike is supposed to destroy the Soviets, assuming they are still putting up a fight, who will hardly expect the ultimate in surprise attacks.

defcon abbreviation for defensive conditions. These range through five levels, from 5 ('apple jack' – normal readiness) to 4 ('lemon juice') through to 1 ('cocked pistol' – maximum force readiness).

demographic targeting the choosing of population centres as targets for nuclear missile and bomber attacks.
See also **countervalue**

denial any aggressive operations directed at securing a military position by placing some form of 'physical' barrier in the way of the enemy; thus, denial of space would mean the immediate destruction of any hostile attempts to place satellites and/or weapons in what was claimed as 'one's own' space-based areas.
See also **deterrence**

denied areas
(1) those areas within the USSR and Warsaw Pact countries which are so situated that they defy simple intelligence gathering techniques, such as human observation on the ground, and must be probed by more complex, usually electronic, methods.
(2) those areas of W. and E. Germany which are denied by the West or the Soviets to the inspection of the opposite party. Such denial is regularly abused, but usually in a sufficiently clandestine manner to maintain the diplomatic fiction of agreement.

dense pack one of the leading possibilities suggested for the basing of the **MX** moveable **ICBM**. One of the main problems contingent on the development of the MX has been its basing; the most recent of these, the **race track** system (or the shell game) and the parallel grid system, were both abandoned in the face of closely spaced basing or dense pack. This envisaged the placing of 100 MX missiles in 100 launch containers which in turn were protected by special hardened capsules; these capsules were to be spaced approximately 1,800–2,200 feet apart over an area of 10–15 square miles. The guiding concept behind dense pack was **fratricide**, the theory that if the mass of MXs required the explosion of a number of missiles to destroy them, these missiles would not only, in their various explosions, destroy each other, or at least their guidance systems, but they would also create such turbulence, fires, gamma rays and similar chaos that there would be no real possibility of a further attack for some two hours. During this time those MXs that had survived, and it was assumed that some would survive, could be launched in retaliation. Dense pack was finally discarded when Congress, in November 1982, refused to vote sufficient funds for a project which seemed, to its detractors, to be making a virtue of vulnerability; dense pack would 'succeed' by attracting a massive blitz of nuclear destruction. Although a number of missiles might ride out the attack, it was wondered whether any of the US would be there to see them. There has yet to emerge a satisfactory basing system for MX.

See also **CSB**

dentology the 'science' of identifying otherwise anonymous black-painted submarines by the dents in a specific hull, the configuration of rivets and other small but potentially significant differences.

See also **cratology**

destruct to destroy a faulty rocket or missile during its flight. Destruct mechanisms are also placed in the sensitive areas of such large military targets as ships, so as to ensure that no secret material is left intact for an enemy in the case of a military defeat.

See also **PAL**

détente an improvement of relations between nations, under which they 'agree to disagree peacefully' (H. Kahn 1962); in the nuclear world this implies a degree of mutual understanding and, possibly, attempts at control or even de-escalation of the arms race. Although President Kennedy could write to Premier Khruschev in 1962, 'If you are prepared to discuss a détente affecting NATO and the Warsaw pact, we are quite prepared to consider . . . any useful proposals,' the US involvement in Vietnam put paid to any such efforts. Thus Richard Nixon, encouraged by the policy's greatest supporter, Dr Henry Kissinger, was able to promote himself as architect of the US–Soviet accords which reached a peak between 1972–3 and are epitomised in the **ABM** treaty of 1972. But Nixon's credibility vanished with Watergate, as did that of *détente* as the new President Ford proved unable to hold off the challenge of hardliners who vilified *détente* as a 'sellout' or 'going to a wife-swapping party and coming home alone'. Despite the continuing popularity of *détente* in Europe – where W. Germany's *Ostpolitik* promotes an accommodation with Russia – President Reagan has made it clear that his foreign policy has no place for *détente*. Russia, to Reagan, is 'the evil empire' and there can be no talks with atheists. In his first press conference he condemned 'the one-way street that the Soviet Union has used to pursue its own ends', notably 'world revolution', a creed against which all Westerners must be prepared to fight. To this end US strategy is dedicated and a new Cold War, 1980s-style, subsequently dominated superpower relations.

deterrence literally 'dissuasion by terror'. Deterrence ('the highest priority task of the strategic forces' (Kahn)) sets out to prevent an enemy from doing something through fear of the consequences that will inevitably follow such an act. Deterrence is in effect psychological – and the metaphors surrounding it refer to chess, bridge and poker – but the threat may require a material backup. Nuclear deterrence – planning not for World War III but to ensure that such hostilities never occur – is based on the possession and deployment of **ICBM**s and **SLBM**s, the heavyweights of the nuclear armoury. The first 'strategic' use of deterrence came in September 1945, when scientists met to discuss the A-bomb attacks on Japan. Professor Jacob Viner stated that 'retaliation in equal terms is unavoidable and in this sense the atomic bomb is a war deterrent, a peace-making force'. Later he elaborated the concept to say that if one power can retaliate in kind against another atomic power, then so can each deter the other from using those weapons. Developed by Viner's student Bernard Brodie in *The Absolute Weapon* (1946), the meaning of deterrence was this: 'Thus far the chief purpose of our military establishment has been to win wars. From now on its chief purpose must be to avoid them. It can have almost no other useful purpose.' Reiterated by former hawk Robert MacNamara in 1982, the premise remains: 'Nuclear weapons are totally useless – except only to deter one's opponent from using them.' In other words, nuclear weapons are too effective to be used but, for deterrence to keep working, massive consumption of human, natural and economic resources must be accepted, all for what has been termed by US historian Theodore Draper 'a nuclear non-strategy' which 'amounts to this: We have nuclear weapons; we are going to have them; but the weapons themselves are of such a nature that we – and other nuclear powers – dare not use them. It is not the most elegant or satisfying solution . . . At best deterrence belongs to the lesser evil, or faute-de-mieux, variety of human conduct.'

As practised by the US today, the policy is in fact 'extended deterrence', the spreading of the US nuclear umbrella beyond its own shores to those of its NATO and European allies. Whether, in event of war, the US would, in the words of one scholar, 'commit suicide on behalf of Western Europe' is of course subject to debate. The ultimate theory of deterrence, depending not on guaranteed armageddon but on the provision of impenetrable, space-based defence, is seen in Mr Reagan's 'Star Wars' (**SDI**) proposal of March 1983. Whether this will work or merely create further militarisation, this time of space, will rest on the fruits of the $30bn+ research funds that the Pentagon is seeking for the project.

Current deterrent policy has been divided by Herman Kahn into six levels. Minimum: a relatively small deterrent which depends as much on nuclear taboos – the 'inconveniences' suffered by both sides, the sanctity of thresholds, and a variety of unreliable attack mechanisms. Workable: a capability of inflicting several million casualties on the enemy and of destroying vital property. 'Adequate': a reliable threat to kill 5–10 per cent of the population. 'Reliable': the killing of more than 33 per cent of the population. Approaching Absolute: the killing of between half and 200 per cent (thus an overkill factor of two) which, for all practical purposes, means 'the end of the world'. Stark: overkill by a factor of ten or more, implying levels of armaments, and the threat implicit in them, that would convince anyone, however adamantly militaristic, that their use would be cataclysmic. In the event, all might succeed, and any could fail, even 'Stark'. It is the belief that 'city-swaps', that would come with 'adequate' deterrence, could be accepted by a nation that underlines the current theories of 'winnable' nuclear wars; the arms levels, undoubtedly, have long reached a 'stark' capability.

See also **denial, MAD**

DEW line acronym for Distant Early Warning line. A system of radar stations on or around the 70th parallel of the N. American continent and at its full extent linking Alaska to Iceland in order to offer some eight hours' warning of approaching nuclear bombers. The system was the most ambitious of those constructed in the 1950s as a defence against surprise Soviet bomber attack. Originally costing $500m and completed in 1962, the system is now well out of date and, under the general plans to modernise the US **C³I** capability, it is scheduled for substantial improvements and will be replaced by the **SEEK FROST** programme. That such ground-based stations remain extremely vulnerable to swift destruction has not influenced Pentagon planners.

See also **BMEWS**

dirty a nuclear explosion that carries the maximum amount of fallout.

See also **ground burst**

discriminating weapons weapons – especially the newest generations of **ICBMs** and **SLBMs** – that can attain sufficient accuracy for military planners to choose only those enemy targets they wish to destroy. This belief, the backbone of **counterforce** targeting and the 'limited' nuclear war it supposes, is presented as a means of sparing civilian population, and as the final answer to the threats of **assured destruction**. In fact it is an illusion. In the first place, so interwoven are the sites of military installations and urban centres that even pinpoint accuracy will kill millions of civilians. In the second place, launching a counterforce **first strike** may limit marginally the civilian deaths amongst one's enemy; however it will only increase them at home, as the retaliatory strike, knowing that silos and airbases would now be empty, would retarget their own attack on cities.

See also **MARV, smart bomb**

D

D

discrimination the ability of an anti-missile weapon to appreciate the difference between a real weapon and the decoys that such a weapon launches to confuse the electronics of its opponents.

Doomsday Clock a clock that is printed on each edition of the *Bulletin of the Atomic Scientists* (founded in 1945 by a group of physicists at the University of Chicago) which tells the 'time' remaining, given the current state of relations between the superpowers, before World War III and the nuclear doomsday. Originally set at 11.52, it has only been turned back once – in 1960 when N. S. Khruschev appeared to be 'thawing' out the Cold War – and now stands at 11.58.

doomsday plane
See also **Looking Glass**

doomsday scenario the 'war games' played by US military planners in an attempt to evaluate possible ways in which a nuclear war might start.
See also **escalation**

dove a person who advocates negotiations as a means of terminating or preventing a military conflict, as opposed to one who advocates a hard-line or warlike policy. Coined by US reporters Stewart Alsop and Charles Bartlett in the *Saturday Evening Post*, 8 December 1962, writing about the Cuban Missile Crisis: 'The hawks favoured an airstrike to eliminate the Cuban missile bases . . . The doves opposed the air strike and favoured a blockade.'
See also **hawk**

dual capable bombers that are made capable of delivering either nuclear or conventional weapons against a target.

dual phenomenology the confirmation, from more than one early warning radar source, of the potential and approaching threat that follows a USSR nuclear missile launch. US forces require such backed-up information before executing defensive and retaliatory measures.
See also **ICBM, NORAD**

dual track originated at a meeting of NATO leaders on Guadeloupe in January 1979. The policy that NATO deployment of new weapons would proceed in parallel to the continuous seeking of arms limitation talks with the Russians to reduce, limit or even eliminate the very weapons that were to be deployed. This concept was spearheaded by France's Giscard d'Estaing, who could not and would not take on any of the new missiles, since France was no longer a NATO member. The Carter Administration seized the idea, soon promoting it as a US initiative and forming two NATO teams: the Special Consultative Group, charged with diplomatic approaches to the USSR; and the High Level Group, which was deploying the weapons. In December 1979 the reports of the HLG and SCG were amalgamated in the Integrated Decision Document (IDD), which in effect institutionalised and codified 'dual track'. The notable parts of the document stressed that negotiations should concentrate on missiles (not airplanes) and that limitations should cover Russian forces facing East as well as West. While the IDD gave the hope that the negotiations might mean that some new US weapons might not need to be deployed if the Soviets played ball, it was always assumed that there must be some deployment, come what may. The idea of **zero option** was as yet inconceivable. Russia responded with its own 'dual track': if the US did not deploy, then Russian Eurostrategic weapons would be frozen, even reduced or pulled back from NATO targets; otherwise arms talks would be abandoned and the build-up accelerated. The US was unimpressed. Only in Europe, especially Germany, did the Russian suggestions catch on. Helmut Schmidt suggested an interim measure – a moratorium on deployments by both sides for three years, i.e. no more SS-20s and no Pershing IIs or Tomahawks whatsoever. Washington was understandably suspicious and Carter wrote to Schmidt, warning him to adhere to dual track. Furious at the rebuke, Schmidt replied 'You can rest assured that you can depend on the bloody Germans!' His interim measure, like all similar attempts to restrict superpower missiles in Europe, went disregarded by all concerned.

See also **INF talks, zero option**

dull sword US Department of Defense Nuclear Accident Code

– any minor, insignificant nuclear incident, rating lower than any accident.

dumb rock a gravity bomb. A bomb without a guidance system, which is simply dropped vertically onto the target below its carrier plane.
See also **iron, smart bomb**

dust defence a missile defence system based on the theory that exploding missiles create enormous volumes of dust and debris, thus interfering with the guidance electronics of incoming missiles. To protect US missiles, devices could be exploded which would create artificial dust storms and thus interfere with Soviet weapons. One of the major schemes investigated for the possible defence of the **MX** missile.

dwarf dud a nuclear weapon that explodes as expected but, after so doing, fails to provide the degree of explosive yield that might be expected from its size.
See also **absolute dud**

E

EAM acronym for Emergency Action Message. The coded Presidential message used for strategic nuclear communications which tells the forces when to attack, when to hold fire and when to cease fire.
See also **football, go-codes, NMCS**

E

ECM electronic counter-measures: a variety of techniques ranging from the simple – the dropping of **metallic chaff** – to the complex – the creation of electronic 'decoy missiles' on hostile radar screens – that are used by missiles and strategic bombers to confuse enemy scanners and early-warning systems.

eighth card the US Department of Defense programme for the development of lasers for military use, both on the ground and in space.

electron overload a theory that hopes to solve the problems of unexplained malfunctions in highly sophisticated electronics systems (especially in warplanes). The proximity of so many electrical circuits fulfilling different functions and the impossibility of ensuring perfect insulation means that one circuit may be activated by a charge from another.

elephant ears large, heavy metal discs added to a rocket or missile both to reinforce it against heat gained through friction in flight and to stabilise the flight orbit.

ELF acronym for extremely low frequency – a communication frequency used for reaching strategic submarines (**SSBN**s). This frequency works on only 2 W radio power, transmits at only one letter every five minutes, and is supposedly inaudible to hostile tracking stations. ELF is the only frequency that can communicate with submarines travelling at operational depths and at cruising speed, *c.* 35 mph, without putting an antenna on the surface. It is by ELF messages that a possible US **first strike**, inevitably involving SSBNs, would be coordinated. The US Navy began researching into ELF in 1958. A variety of schemes have been planned since then. One system, soon rejected, was to use the existing 850-mile powerline between Los Angeles and Oregon as a gigantic antenna–transmitter. In 1969 an ELF Test Facility was built at Clam Lake, Wisconsin. This set up two 14-mile-long antennae which were successful in contacting submerged submarines. Attempts to create a full-scale operational ELF facility have continually run into opposition. The need to bury the antennae – initially proposed as a grid of 2,400 miles of cable dug in some 6 feet below the ground over a 4,700-square-mile area of Michigan – so as to survive a missile attack brought fears as to the environmental and physical damage such works might cause. ELF was rejected in Michigan, Wisconsin and Texas before the current Project ELF was accepted. This version, with only 56 miles of antenna connected to the Clam Lake facility to make a total of 84 miles, will be able to communicate with submarines in at least a half of the world's oceans. It is assumed that this modest beginning will be expanded. It is possible that a supposed US 'weather station' in Alice Springs, Australia, is in fact a second ELF facility, providing communications with the other half of the globe.

elint abbreviation for electronic intelligence. The monitoring, measuring, identifying and analysing of all varieties of hostile communications and radar activity. Such information, gathered by satellite, airplane, ship and ground installations, is referred to the National Security Agency, Fort Meade, Maryland, processed by **Deaf-smack** and used for the analysis of the Soviet 'order of battle', the development of electronic counter-measures against hostile **C³I** and, based on this overview of Soviet 'intentions and capabilities', the planning of the US 'order of battle' and the selecting of hostile targets. Elint developed in the 1950s, typified by the U2 'spy flights' and the chain of listening posts set up around the borders of the USSR. The first elint satellite, a 1-ton spacecraft, was launched in 1962; three large-scale successors followed in 1963, 1968 and 1970, each weighing between 3,300 and 4,400 lb. Lightweight surveillance satellites first arrived in 1963 – the 120-lb 'ferrets' which 'hitchhiked' along the orbits of photo-reconnaissance satellites. The latest of these is the KH-11, designed specifically to monitor Soviet **ICBM** tests. While such satellites offer excellent viewing facilities (with the exception of the DSP (Defence Support Programme) satellites which maintain a geosynchronous orbit and thus stay in the same place above the earth as it rotates), their main failure is a lack of 'real-time' immediacy. Restricted to the periods – six to eight minutes each – during which they pass over a ground station and can dump their information, they still cannot offer the 'instant' facts on Soviet troop activities, so vital for decision-making during an actual crisis or war.

See also **comint, humint, sigint, telint**

emanations the electronic pulses that can be monitored by a variety of elint listening posts and which indicate radar activity among hostile forces, anti-aircraft emplacements, ships, etc. Listeners for such emanations monitor any exceptional RFs (radio frequencies), PRFs (pulse repetition frequencies) or series of commands or inter-troop transmissions which make up the **EOB** (electronic order of battle) and relay them to the National Security Agency in Fort Meade, Maryland, for detailed analysis and processing.

See also **elint, EW**

emergency action message

See **EAM**

EMP acronym for electro-magnetic pulse. The result of nuclear explosion – the release of intense bursts of energy across the electro-magnetic spectrum. These bursts can temporarily or permanently damage or destroy all kinds of electronic equipment, both on the ground and in space, and could be fatal to satellites as well as earth communications systems. It is quite feasible that the EMP alone that results from a **first strike** impact would be sufficient, irrespective of the concomitant and devastating heat and blast damage, to wreck the greater proportion of the US **SIOP**, as well as such civil defence and similar non-military communications that might be necessary to sustain some form of organised life under attack.

enable to arm a weapon preparatory to use; especially to arm a missile with its nuclear warhead(s).

endurance the ability to fight and control a nuclear war over a period of time.

enhanced radiation weapon (*or* neutron bomb) first developed *c.* 1957 by Edward Teller, the neutron bomb was designed to create a 'clean' nuclear weapon without the massive fallout that characterised the then current developments. Teller's weapon could even be used for civilian purposes, e.g. quick and enormous excavations, with no harm to human beings. It was pointed out by Linus Pauling, and subsequently by Andrei Sakharov, that the millions of neutrons released by the bomb would combine with the nitrogen in the air to form carbon-14, a deadly and almost infinitely persistent form of radiation, producing cancers and genetic defects for generations. The project was shelved until 1974, when it reappeared in a new guise. The intention now was to maximise the high radiation, combined with relatively minimal (to an **ICBM**) blast and heat damage to create an ideal theatre nuclear weapon. Exploded *c.* 300 feet above a battlefield, it would knock out tank crews but, weighing a mere one kiloton, would create minimal destruction of *materiel*. In the event, the real drawback was that even heavily irradiated crews would take some hours to die, thus making their use of strategic weapons a real possibility. But the downfall of the neutron bomb came through a supremely bungled public relations exercise; it appeared to most people that America was proposing a bomb that killed people and left buildings intact. However inaccurate such theories might be, they shocked the uninitiated masses and the bomb was shelved again. That it will eventually, if surreptitiously, be deployed is in little doubt but, like the universally deplored chemical weapons, the neutron bomb remains among the most unacceptable faces of an otherwise paradoxically tolerated situation.

EOB acronym for electronic order of battle. A top secret catalogue of Soviet radars sited along the Soviet coasts and borders and from ships and aircraft, which is compiled to create a

comprehensive survey of Soviet air defences for use by US bomber crews.
See also **elint**

ER acronym for enhanced radiation.
See also **enhanced radiation weapon**

ERCS acronym for Emergency Rocket Communications System. In the event of all other US land- and air-based communications systems being destroyed, a number of Minuteman **ICBMs** are fitted with radio transmitters instead of warheads. Once launched on the orders of the surviving US leadership flying on board the NEACP (**Kneecap**), these rockets are programmed to broadcast from many miles high those orders that will command strategic submarines – assumed to have survived a Soviet first strike – to fire their weapons.

error budget the factors which together contribute to an assessment of the probable accuracy of a missile. These include variations in the earth's gravitational field, the technical limitations of the guidance system, the imprecision of rocket fuel burn rates, the effects of the atmosphere on re-entering warheads, the exactness of the estimations of the relative locations of launch site and target.
See also **CEP**

escalation a military coinage as early as 1938, but popularised by nuclear futurologist Herman Kahn (born 1922) in the 1950s and 1960s. The concept of a build-up of military forces and inter-power conflict that leads from minor crisis through a series of major crises and thence to nuclear war, itself developing in intensity from merely 'exemplary' explosions, probably on theatre troops, to full-scale no-holds-barred, no targets excluded, **spasm war**. In his book *Thinking About the Unthinkable* (1962) Kahn explained: 'There is a tendency for each side to counter the other's pressure with a somewhat stronger one of its own. This increasing pressure step by step is called "escalation"' or, as defined by Thomas C. Schnelling, 'a competition in risk-taking'. In all escalation two sets of basic elements co-exist and interplay: the political, diplomatic and military issues surrounding the particular conflict; and the level of violence and provocation at which it is fought. Whether or not the escalation proceeds inexorably to cataclysm or whether the process can be reversed (**escalation control**) depends on this complex of relationships.

See also **brinkmanship, escalation control, escalation dominance, escalation ladder**

escalation control (*or* de-escalation) a concept central to contemporary ideas of 'winnable' and 'limited' nuclear wars. The belief that the escalation of such wars – even after the missiles have been fired – can still be held in check. De-escalation from the lower rungs of Kahn's **escalation ladder** seems feasible – the stepping back from any crisis that threatens the use of nuclear weapons is likely to be greeted with relief, albeit with the proviso that something must be done to make sure that such an event does not recur (and that 'something' need by no means be simply appeasement). Once the crises have reached the upper rungs (past Kahn's 'No Nuclear Use Threshold') such de-escalation as there may be will be against the background of massive destruction and death. In that event it is to be wondered whether either side would be able or willing to claim a 'victory'. Kahn himself, in *Thinking About the Unthinkable* (1962) suggested that only then, in the awful aftermath, might there be formed a world government.

See also **austere wars, crisis management**

escalation dominance the theory that, all things being equal, one side must possess the **capability** to mount the **escalation ladder** one step ahead of the opponent and thus reach the top, or at least the highest rung, prior to de-escalation (**escalation control**) in the dominant position. Escalation dominance is 'a function of where one is on the . . . ladder. It depends on the net effect of the competing capabilities on the rung being occupied, the estimate by each side of what would happen if the confrontation moved to other rungs and the means each side has to shift the confrontation to these other rungs' (Kahn, 1962). There is also the edge gained by that side which least fears 'eruption' (the actual outbreak of war) anywhere on the ladder. Escalation dominance is perhaps the area of international relations that most resembles the poker bluff.

escalation ladder proposed in Herman Kahn's *On Escalation* (1965) is 'a generalised or abstract scenario' (for nuclear war), an 'escalation ladder', described as 'a linear arrangement of roughly increasing levels of intensity of crisis' divided into forty-four 'rungs', grouped themselves in seven categories, moving through six thresholds. From rung 1 (ostensible crisis) to rung 44 (spasm or insensate war) the progress of a putative World War III runs from Sub-Crisis Manoeuvring (Don't Rock the Boat Threshold) to Traditional Crises (Nuclear War is Unthinkable Threshold) to Intense Crises (No Nuclear Use Threshold) to Bizarre Crises (Central Sanctuary Threshold) to Exemplary Central Attacks (Central War Threshold) to Military Central Wars (City Targeting Threshold) to Civilian Central Wars and thence to Aftermath. Kahn stresses that 'escalation ladders are metaphorical tools that have been found useful in preliminary studies of escalation. No particular ladder should be considered as being a theory of international relations . . . its utility derives partly from its provision of a convenient list of some of the options available . . . and partly from its ordering of escalatory activities in a way that facilitates examination and discussion.' While such ladders tend to refer to the Western side of the confrontation, the Soviet system is equally susceptible to such theorising. Taking assumptions based on the Marxist-Leninist concepts of subordinating military to political action and the importance of ideology in foreign policy, such Soviet ladders contain an initial set of rungs grouped as 'Political and Psychological Warfare' and 'Violence by Proxy' that precede more general escalation.

See also **escalation**

ESI acronym for extremely sensitive information. A super-secret classification code used only for matters pertaining to the US **SIOP**.

ET acronym for emergent technology. The increasingly sophisticated application of laser and chip technology to battlefield weapons, both conventional and nuclear. ET radically enhances accuracy, speed, etc., for weapons used by individual infantrymen.

event

(1) the site of a nuclear test.

(2) an accidental failure or breakdown in any nuclear device, including military weapons and civilian reactors or power plants.

EW acronym for electronic warfare. 'The use of a wide range of electronic systems and subsystems to conduct active or passive measurement of an enemy's offensive or defensive electronic capabilities, attack or defend against those systems, and reach tactical or strategic mission objectives using personnel and/or weapons that include ground forces, ships, submarines, aircraft and missiles' (C. Campbell, 1982). Consuming 33 per cent of the USAF annual equipment costs, EW also counts for 25 per cent of the research budget, exceeding that for weapons, aircraft or propulsion. The USAF Systems Command runs 40,000 computers and 250,000 other '**black boxes**'. The refinements of increasingly complex electronics technology have created an 'electronic order of battle' (**EOB**) which extends from ground to air and beneath the sea. As well as providing the electronics to run the electronic battlefield, EW concentrates on ECM (electronic counter-measures – essentially jamming enemy electronics), ECCM (electronic counter counter-measures – jamming the enemy's jamming) and ESM (electronic support measures – the gathering and analysing of any details pertaining to hostile EW technology). EW also extends into intelligence gathering, using a mass of satellites, listening posts and computers to obtain and process the volume of information so obtained.

See also **C³CM, C³I, comint, elint, humint, sigint, telint**

F

fade out US Department of Defense level 1 war readiness. Every commander is ordered to act for himself in the ultimate stage of nuclear combat.

FAE acronym for fuel-air weapon.
See also **cheeseburger**

fail safe the concept in international relations whereby nuclear war may not be triggered 'by accident' or by a lone psychotic. US bombers have a 'fail-safe point' to which they fly in the case of a given level of war readiness alert, but which they must not pass unless specifically ordered; this permits the checking of whether or not the emergency must lead to war – for instance if a reported hostile **first strike** is already on its way. If possible the bombers are ordered back; once they pass the fail-safe point, each individual commander is supposed to deliver his bombs on target. There exists no similar check on **ICBMs** – once launched there is no way of recalling them, a fact that is brought into increasing focus by the computerisation of many US early-warning and command systems which may be planned to eliminate human error but, likewise, offer no constraint on mechanical malfunction.
See also **attack options, dual phenomenology**

fallback the material – earth, human and building remains, etc. – that is blown into the air by a nuclear explosion and which ultimately, and after contamination by radioactive fallout, returns to the earth.
See also **fallout**

fallout the radioactive refuse of a nuclear bomb explosion and the process of the deposition of such refuse on the surrounding land and human and animal population. The extent of this fallout differs as to the type of explosion: an **air burst** will be limited as to local effects, but with the greater dispersion into the atmosphere will have far greater potential as a global pollutant; a **ground zero** burst will irradiate dust and water droplets and form a lethal fallout cloud that will stay close to the ground and become subject to dispersal by prevailing winds. A one-megaton **surface burst** carried by a 15 mph wind would poison people with doses of between 3,000 and 90 rems over an area 150 miles long and 20 miles wide over a period of seven days (a dose of 250–450 rems will kill at least 50 per cent of those exposed). There is also a short pulse of direct, immediate radiation accompanying a nuclear blast. Radiation attacks lymphoid tissue, bone marrow, spleen, testes and the gastrointestinal tract as electrons already in the tissue absorb and interact with the radiation – the greater the dose, the greater the damage. However if the time of exposure is extended and the dose less immediately concentrated, the damage to the tissues should be less since cells recover in parallel to receiving new radiation. Although the authorities have been aware of the problems of radiation since Wilhelm Roentgen discovered X-rays in 1895, the constant philosophy has been one of disinformation, euphemism and simple lies, accompanied by a modicum of cosmetic civil defence projects. Protection comes a poor second to progress and the arms race brooks no hindrance on humanitarian grounds. In 1974 the US prepared a scenario illustrating the consequences of a Soviet **counterforce** attack comprising 2,158 air-bursting missiles: as well as 6.7m immediate deaths, there would be 5.1m sufferers from radiation sickness; long-term radiation effects would include up to 30,000 neoplasm deaths per year for several years; 8,000 leukaemia deaths per year for several years; 5,000–10,000 genetic deaths per year for a generation; an average life shortening of 0.7 years; 20,000 congenital malformation deaths out of an assumed 3m pregnancies affected by the attack. Such figures were considered conservative; they would also be vastly magnified in a **countervalue** strike on cities, in which the immediate deaths alone would number 90m or more civilians. Non-fatal long-term effects – anaemia, cataracts, retarded development, non-fatal malformations in foetuses – were also not included. In an assumed 200-warhead attack on the UK (the number estimated in the government's Square Leg exercise (1980) as likely, given the potential targets in the UK), deaths would number 29m, with an additional 6.4m immediate casualties, not counting long-term victims of fallout and disease.

Fat Man the second atomic bomb, used to destroy Nagasaki at 11.02 am on 9 August 1945. The bomb measured 3 metres and weighed 4,500 kilograms. It was exploded in an **air burst** 500 metres above the city and had a yield of some 22,000 tons (22 KT) of TNT.

FBS acronym for forward based systems. A term coined by Soviet negotiators to describe those US forces – other than **ICBMs** – such as missiles based in NATO countries, on allied territory, or on submarines or aircraft carriers, all of which are capable of delivering a nuclear strike against Russia. Given the relative geography of the West and the Warsaw Pact, the USSR has no such forward bases of its own. Thus these systems are seen as giving the US an unfair advantage and as such appear as a major bargaining chip at arms talks, epitomised by periodic Soviet suggestions of a 'freeze' – promises to restrict deployment of its own weapons if the US will keep new missiles, specifically **cruise**, out of Europe.

FEBA acronym for forward edge of the battle area. That area of a battlefield where the opposing forces are actually facing and fighting each other in reasonably close contact.

fellow traveller a satellite-conveyed nuclear mine that would be launched to 'shadow' its target – a laser weapon or communications/surveillance satellite – and which could be exploded when desired by ground-based computer commands, thus destroying that target.

See also **SBL**

Fencer the Russian Sukhoi SU-24 supersonic, swing-wing nuclear-capable attack aircraft, first deployed in 1974. The Fencer is the approximate equivalent to the US F-111, although it carries only 50 per cent of the F-111's payload. Its combat radius is *c.* 1,100 miles, although with a full payload of ten bombs and two extra fuel tanks, this is reduced to 400 miles (reduced by a further 50 per cent when flying close to the ground, where the air is 'thicker' and drag higher). Some 800 aircraft have been produced. The Fencer is particularly admired in the West for its all-weather avionics systems, permitting its pilot to aim bombs accurately despite darkness or poor weather, and has been cited as 'perhaps the greatest threat to Western Europe' by the *International Defense Review*. Sceptics are less impressed; the Fencer resembles the F-111, they feel, in only its major faults.

See also **Fishbed, Fitter A, Fitter D/H, Flogger D/J**

final order the last command to military leaders from the President or other surviving authority, ordering them to take individual responsibility for their own actions, to fire weapons at will and let each man act for himself. Such an order is reserved for the final stages of a world locked in **spasm war**.

See also **fade out**

F

finite deterrence a war plan considered by the Eisenhower and Kennedy administrations in which US nuclear forces were stripped down to a fleet of (as near as possible) invulnerable strategic and hunter-killer submarines. Political, military and industrial pressures ended this plan, although it was briefly, if abortively, disinterred by President Carter, himself an ex-submariner, in the late 1970s.

fire and forget any missile that has a self-guiding **smart** internal computer that will steer it towards its target with no further assistance from the launcher and which thus once fired can be 'forgotten'.

See also **free rocket**

firebreak from the forestry term, a bare strip of land between woods, intended to suppress the spread of fires. Thus in military usage it is the theoretical gap between the capability and use of conventional weapons and the launching of a full-scale nuclear war. Given the strategic doctrines of the superpowers, this gap is now generally seen to have been eroded to virtually nothing.

See also **escalation ladder**

first strike the first offensive move of a war. In nuclear terms, the successful first strike implies the ability to eliminate **retaliation** by the enemy by **counterforce** targeting. Thus first-strike capability – the ability of a nuclear power to attack hostile missile silos with nuclear first-strike weapons, thereby reducing or eliminating its ability to retaliate. The essential first-strike weapon is the **ICBM** which, with its speed and accuracy of delivery, can be used for a pre-emptive attack, while slower bombers or **cruise missiles** (although the Soviets refute this difference at arms talks, claiming that cruise, when deployed in Europe, is too near for the speed to matter) forfeit that element of surprise required of any first strike. Though both powers reject any idea of their own launch of a first strike, much of the arms race depends on projecting the belief that the other side is waiting only for the chance to attack. Perceptions of the other side's weapons programmes can only add to this mutual distrust. While the US stresses that every technological advance is merely to keep pace with the Soviets, they in turn claim that such developments as the super-accurate **MARV** or the **Trident** II missile (the first **SLBM** to threaten hard targets), as well as the supposedly invulnerable 'Star Wars' technology (**SDI**), for all that Mr Reagan has proposed sharing this space-based development with the Soviets, are all designed to give the US an unassailable first-strike capability, admitted or not.

See also **survivability**

first use the first use in a war of a specific level of weapons or type of military measure. Thus, if a **first strike** were conventional then a second strike with nuclear weapons would still be a first use of such armaments. Neither superpower will admit that it would use nuclear weapons first. In 1982 and 1983 groups of concerned experts in America and the UK demanded that their respective governments should adopt an official 'no first use' policy, thus putting some real weight behind the pious declarations. To date, neither government has shown an interest in such a move.

Fishbed the Russian MiG-21 nuclear-capable strike aircraft. Designed initially to counter the high-flying B-47 and B-52 bombers, the MiG-21 is probably the most widely deployed aircraft in the world today. The nuclear capable version was first deployed in the early 1970s and 100 remain in service. It carries a 2000 lb payload – conventional or nuclear – over a 300-mile combat radius. The MiG-21 is often cited as an exemplar of Soviet design simplicity and operations reliability, and is internationally popular, but the easily interchangeable parts are subject to wear, the engine has an unduly short life, and the handling is by no means foolproof, even clumsy. The MiG's combat record seems to vary as to adversary; the Israelis knocked out twenty MiGs for every one of their own losses flying against the Syrians in 1982, but the N. Vietnamese used the MiG successfully against the ultra-modern US aircraft over Vietnam.

See also **Fencer, Fitter A, Fitter D/H, Flogger D/J**

F

fission 'The splitting, either spontaneously or under the impact of another particle, of a heavy nucleus into two (very rarely three or more) approximately equal parts, with resulting release of large amounts of energy' (*OED Supplement*, 1972). For fission to occur the atomic particle must be unstable, i.e. the nuclear binding forces within it must be unable to hold it together. In the original A-bombs uranium-235 or plutonium-239 were used as the fissile material. Fission is produced when a neutron enters the nucleus of an atom of one of these materials, which then breaks up. A large amount of energy is released, the original nucleus splits into two radioactive nuclei (the **fission products**) and two or three neutrons are produced. It is then possible to continue this process in a self-sustaining chain reaction if at least one of the neutrons released in each fission in turn produces another fission reaction. The smallest amount of the material in which this self-sustaining chain reaction – which causes the actual nuclear explosion – can be made to occur is called the critical mass. This depends on the nuclear properties of the material used for the fission process. The higher the density of the material, the shorter distance a neutron needs to travel before triggering the next fission, and thus the smaller the critical mass. Fission is initiated by compressing a mass that is slightly less than critical into one that is slightly greater than critical. The chain reaction thus caused reaches a climax in half of one millionth of a second, after fifty-five 'generations' of sub-division. This number of generations must be achieved if the nuclear explosion is to take place, and the fissile material must be held together for the short period that will ensure that this happens. The explosion itself generates intense heat and ultra-high pressures, as well as expanding the fissile material at 1000 km per second (651 miles per second). Two methods of triggering the A-bombs that exploded over Japan were used. The 'gun' method (Hiroshima) involved the firing towards each other of two sub-critical hemispheres of nuclear material – when these collided they produced the necessary critical mass. The compression of a sub-critical into a critical mass – the 'implosion' method – was used at Nagasaki, the compression being performed by the explosion of a casing of TNT around the fissile material. This latter method is used in today's bombs since it is the most efficient in its use of fissionable material.

See also **fusion, fission–fusion–fission**

fission products the 300 or more different isotopes which can be formed when fission takes place.

See also **fission**

fission–fusion–fission a three-stage thermonuclear bomb with a uranium or fission trigger, a hydrogen or fusion intermediate stage and an outer case of 'natural' uranium.

See also **fission, fusion**

Fitter A the senior Russian nuclear-capable strike aircraft, the Sukhoi SU-7. The plane has been in service since 1960, with 150 still deployed in the mid-1980s. It has a combat radius of 400 miles and carries a 2.5 ton bomb payload.

See also **Fencer, Fishbed, Flogger D/J**

Fitter D/H the Russian Sukhoi SU-17 swing-wing ground attack fighter. Introduced in 1974, the aircraft carries a maximum weapons load of 5 tons over a combat radius of 500+ miles. The fleet in 1985 numbered 650.

See also **Fencer, Fishbed, Flogger D/J**

Flanker the Russian SU-27 nuclear-capable strike aircraft, scheduled for deployment by 1990. A similar plane to the US F-15, the Flanker will be deployed initially as an interceptor, then as a strike aircraft.

See also **Fulcrum**

flexible response (*or* gradual deterrence) the concept of meeting aggression with a suitable level of counter-aggression and in the relevant environment; always, unless the initial aggression is a nuclear **first strike**, leaving the options of **escalation** and de-escalation (**escalation control**) available if required or feasible. First accepted by NATO forces in Europe in 1967, the doctrine supposed a battle in the Central Sector (the border of the two Germanies). NATO forces would attempt to hold off the Soviets, using either **conventional** or **tactical nuclear weapons**, until the US was forced to join in, if only by threatening nuclear conflict. In 1961 Robert MacNamara called for 'a policy of controlled flexible response whereby the military forces of the United States would become a finely tuned instrument of national policy'. By 1974 President Nixon's National Security Advisers Henry Kissinger and James Schlesinger formulated the policy with direct reference to the US **SIOP**. Developed from the 'Doctrine of Sufficiency' (an attack that was enough to deter the Soviets but not to rouse them to nuclear retaliation), National Security Decision Memorandum 242 (NSDM-242) encapsulated the new alternative to **MAD**. In future the US would respond as and when a crisis required, with the emphasis on **theatre** conflicts and exemplary actions rather than global cataclysm. The US would, of course, still win. Such a policy, with its assumptions of Soviet restraint, and the pious belief that a nuclear war really can be limited, remains theoretical as to its application. The more practical result, with the formulation of a new SIOP, SIOP-5, incorporating the new options, was the development of new weapons to capitalise on the new philosophy.

Flexible response can appear most seductive: it makes no pre-conditions; its flexibility means that there is neither a promise to go nuclear, nor need there be any restriction on so doing. In the event this is illusory – by making no suggestion as to which sort of war should best be prepared for, it forces military planners to accept that they cannot prepare for any war. Since they must, however, be ready for some level of conflict, they make a choice, and that choice is for nuclear exchange. Even gradual deterrence must possess the essential of any deterrence – the threat of destruction or, in this case, the use of US might in a European theatre, must be seen as real. From the other side, Soviet planning has made it clear that even in the early stages of such a war, when only European theatre warheads were in use, they would respond by a full-scale inter-continental attack on **CONUS**. It would seem, therefore, that since nuclear weapons exist, however delicate may be the theories of limited, flexible war-fighting, the result will remain the same – World War III.

See also **countervailing strategy**

Flogger D/J the Russian MiG-27 nuclear-capable strike aircraft. A swing-wing supersonic plane, carrying a 3.5 ton weapons load over a combat radius of 400 miles. Most versions of the Flogger were developed as interceptors, but some 650, in two ground-attack versions, have been deployed since 1971. The Flogger has been touted as an all-weather fighter-bomber, but its laser beam look-down system cannot pierce the moisture that is usually indicative of European weather, and its vaunted 'electro-optical system' is no more or less than a TV camera, similarly restricted by poor visibility.

See also **Fencer, Fishbed, Fitter A, Fitter D/J**

FLTSATCOM acronym for Fleet Satellite Communications. A network of USN communications satellites administered by the Naval Space Command since 1983. It comprises four spacecraft in geosynchronous orbit (an orbit, usually that of a communications satellite, in which the vehicle moves at the same rate as the earth does, fixed at an altitude of 22,000 miles above the equator) that provide global communications for ships, anti-submarine warfare (**ASW**) planes and other mobile forces, including strategic air force communications. These satellites have twenty-three UHF channels of which nine are used for inter-navy links, one for the Department of Defense and the remainder for the USAF. It is intended that the US Army may in due course be able to join the network. They are considered the most sophisticated of currently orbiting satellites. Despite this excellence, FLTSATCOM may well be replaced by **MILSTAR**.

See also **AFSATCOM**

flush on warning in the case of receiving a warning of incoming missiles, an order to all those aircraft threatened by

the attack to take off at once so as to avoid being destroyed on the ground or within fatal range of the explosions.
See also **attack options**

FOBS acronym for Fractional Orbit Bombardment System.
(1) A strategy of missile attack in which rockets are fired in a low earth orbit (*c.* 100 metres) and on approaching the target are forced out of the orbit and down to the earth by the firing of retro-rockets. This is intended to keep the missiles beneath radar spotting and allied defensive retaliation until the last available moment.
(2) A missile attack that comes 'the wrong way round' the globe, i.e. as far as US planners are concerned, from the south rather than over the North Pole.

F

follow-on theory the concept whereby the completion of work on one **weapons system** is immediately followed by the starting up of work on its successor. A concept that lies at the heart of the continuing arms race, based on a mutually convenient, self-sustaining agreement between the military's various units, which need the latest generation of weapons to justify their existence, and the manufacturers, who need orders to stay in profit.

football the attaché case in which the President's copy of the day's nuclear **go codes** the **SIOP** options and the President's decision book (which contains the President's instructions to authorise the release of nuclear weapons and execute the war plan) are carried. An officer carrying the football stays constantly with the President.
See also **EAM**

footprint the pattern into which it is estimated the various warheads delivered by a **MIRV**-ed **ICBM** should fall on impacting at their targets.
See also **CEP**

force multipliers the premise that what one lacks in quantity, one makes up for in quality. Thus in military terms the use of satellites for reconnaissance, navigation, weather forecasting and communications all in ways that improve the effectiveness of military forces.

Fortress America the concept, beloved of the American right wing, of a nation so well defended – especially by a nuclear strike-force – that whatever happens elsewhere, it will survive unscathed behind such defences.
See also **SDI**

foxhole strength the minimum unit of military strength: one man with one gun positioned in a small defensive hole he has dug himself.

fratricide the concept that if too many missiles are fired together at too concentrated a target or targets, the effects of the initial explosions would be to destroy, disable or deflect by heat, blast and **EMP** those missiles that followed. It is this concept that was put forward to support the now discarded policy of **dense pack** basing of **MX** missiles; fratricide was supposed to leave at least a proportion of the target MXs intact, these survivors then to be launched as a retaliatory strike.
See also **CSB, dense pack**

free rocket a missile that is controlled neither by a launch computer nor by wire guidance but by internal computerised guidance systems.
See also **fire and forget**

Fulcrum the Russian MiG-29 nuclear-capable strike aircraft. Introduced in late 1983, this multi-role fighter-strike aircraft is seen as the likely replacement for the MiG-27 **Flogger D/J**.
See also **Flanker**

full generation a total war footing, with an aggressive potential of 10,000 nuclear weapons.

fusion 'The formation of a heavier, more complex nucleus by the coming together of two or more lighter ones, usually accompanied by the release of relatively large amounts of energy' (*OED Supplement*, 1972). Where the fission-based A-bomb depends on the fission of a single heavy nucleus, the H-bomb is created by the fusion of two light nuclei. This is created by using either deuterium (which has a hydrogen nucleus plus an additional neutron; it is an isotope of hydrogen, also known as hydrogen-2) or tritium (with two additional neutrons; it is also an isotope of hydrogen, known as hydrogen-3). A core of these materials is ignited by the explosion of an atomic bomb, whose radiation is focussed by a packing of styrofoam explosive around the core. This explosion creates the necessary heat (10m degrees C) to fuse the deuterium and tritium nuclei and cause the H-bomb to explode. If, as is usual in US bombs, an additional casing of uranium-238 is put around the core nuclei, a fission–fusion–fission device is created; the U-238 absorbs the neutrons created by the fusion process and undergoes fission itself. The end product of this complex of explosions is a very highly radioactive (**dirty**) bomb. If the U-238 casing is omitted, the basic H-bomb is known as a **neutron bomb**. The H-bomb is far more sophisticated in design (as well as powerful in use) than the A-bomb. The main difficulty is preventing the A-bomb trigger from destroying the entire device long enough for fusion – and the resulting explosion – to take place. The weapon is infinitely more efficient than its predecessors: the Nagasaki weapon produced a **yield-to-weight ratio** of 5,000:1; contemporary warheads are expected to produce 3.5 million:1.

See also **fission, fission–fusion–fission**

G

Galosh the ABM1-B Galosh interceptor, the Soviet nuclear-armed ballistic missile defence system. The Galosh system was first deployed around Moscow subsequent to their introduction in 1964. Sixty-four missiles were in place, in eight batteries of eight missiles each. The Galosh is the only ABM system deployed either by the US or USSR, as permitted by the ABM Treaty of 1972 and the Protocol of 1974. Half the missiles were dismantled by 1980, leaving only four sites. Galosh can carry a nuclear warhead over a range of 200 miles, but suffers from a variety of problems, notably the fact that were only one missile to destroy its target, the explosion caused would create both a massive electro-magnetic pulse (**EMP**) which would wreck the power grid and thus military communications, and would also jam every radar system with the cloud of electronically charged particles that would be released into the air. A new Galosh system may well be being prepared for deployment by 1990, incorporating a large phased-array radar system with 360° coverage. This programme may also be linked to a two-missile system which, if limited to a total of 100 interceptors, would still be acceptable under the ABM treaty.

See also **ABM, PVO Strany**

garage US intelligence term for the hardened defences which defend the launch sites of Soviet SS-20 missiles, the approximate equivalents to US **cruise missiles**.

general war (*or* central war) an all-out war in which all forces are engaged and each superpower makes a series of strikes against the other and its allies. The US Army and USN use 'general', the USAF uses 'central'.

GEODSS acronym for Ground-Based Electro-Optical Deep Space Surveillance. An ultra-fast space-based surveillance system, employed in the surveillance of satellite movements and characteristics, which has substituted an on-board TV camera for the former telescope-style film cameras. The two operators at a GEODSS earth station are therefore capable of near-simultaneous spotting and analysis – with computer processing – of the satellite, its origins, its orbit and of making a comparison of these factors with previous data. The first GEODSS station – at White Sands Missile Range, New Mexico – opened in 1981. Four more are planned, in Korea, in Hawaii and at unannounced sites in the eastern Atlantic and the Middle East.

See also **MHIV, PMALS**

GLCM (*or* glickem) acronym for ground launched cruise missile.

See **cruise missiles**

go codes US military command codes that must be transmitted in the event of launching a nuclear war or responding to a pre-emptive **first strike**. These codes, which change daily, are carried by an officer who must never leave the President's side, in a briefcase known as the **football**. Only on receiving these codes, which have to be matched with relevant counter-codes and a variety of allied security devices, can US nuclear missiles be launched.

gold-plating the habit indulged in by the Pentagon of attaching every conceivable piece of arms or avionics gadgetry to aerospace equipment that has already been commissioned. Such embellishments are always justified in the name of extra combat efficiency, but they rarely bear in mind any form of economic restraint.

See also **baroque armaments**

GPS acronym for Global Positioning System. An ultra-sophisticated guidance system, based on an atomic clock accurate to one second in 30,000 years, for the absolutely accurate navigation and positioning of satellites.

See also **NAVSTAR**

graceful degradation the concept inherent in positing a possibly 'winnable', 'limited' nuclear war, that one's own command, control and communications facilities, and the weapons that they administer, will survive longer, or at least collapse less speedily, than those of the enemy. They will thus continue (albeit damaged) to work to a greater effect than those of the enemy. It is accepted that massive loss and destruction on both sides will accompany this process; thus it would seem that such a victory would merely go to the side that was the last to die of its wounds. Under current US policies, the US would maintain a **second-strike counterforce** capability which could survive the immediate first and retaliatory strikes and, waiting until all other forces seemed on the verge of collapse, would act as the 'secure reserve force' which would gain final success. It is for such a plan that the **MX** missile, supposedly more flexible than silo-based **ICBMs**, is required. Alongside this is the massive **C³I** programme, designed to maintain US communications in any event.

See also **survivability**

grade creep the increase in middle-level officers – 'white-collar' military technicians – which has grown up alongside the development of increasingly sophisticated **weapons systems**.

gradualism escalation towards war that is directly linked to the progress, or rather lack of progress, in gradually disintegrating negotiations.

greenhouse effect a theory of post-nuclear civilisation whereby the effect of multiple explosions would have caused the ozone layer in the atmosphere to be destroyed and would thus permit the harmful rays of the sun to penetrate. The result of this would be akin to living in a superheated greenhouse; water supplies would dry up, plants would 'burn' away and humanity would duly collapse without vital liquids and crops.

See also **nuclear winter**

GRIT acronym for graduated reciprocated reduction in tension. The strategic version of 'turning the other cheek', a version of conflict management that implies not weakness but the desire to avoid all-out conflict and initiate some process of de-escalation. GRIT was developed in 1962 by US professor of psychology

Charles E. Osgood in his book *An Alternative to War or Surrender*. Under a GRIT scenario, the major problems of international relations – notably the weapons themselves – should be put aside, and nations should concentrate on removing lesser, but more easily accessible, sources of tension. The intent of GRIT is to draw from the opponent a similar degree of restraint, pulling further and faster away from the potential war. Obviously the side who initiates such measures takes some risk, and must be prepared to take remedial action in case the enemy attempts to capitalise on such apparent 'softness', but above all diversity and flexibility should typify this style of foreign relations. And in every case there should be a definite suggestion of reciprocity, as well as the offer of simple verification of any measures taken.

ground burst a nuclear explosion that occurs at ground level, or in which the fireball touches the ground. While an **air burst** maximises heat and blast over a large area, the ground burst, creating a fireball that sucks up vast quantities of earth and debris from the crater it has caused, returning them to the earth as radioactive particles, creates a far 'dirtier' effect with this fallout. Ground bursts may well be used for **counterforce** targets, where pinpoint accuracy against military installations is more important than the devastation of a vast area (although the massive radiation thus caused will certainly take its toll, albeit over a longer period).

See also **air burst**

ground zero that part of the target that is situated directly under an exploding nuclear weapon or, in the case of a ground burst, that point on the earth where the missile impacts.

See also **hypocentre**

growler a satellite communications link which is used to provide secure communications that cannot be monitored by hostile land-based scanning and listening stations.

H

HALO acronym for High Altitude Large Optics. A programme still in development by **DARPA** to create a space platform carrying an optical structure some 100 feet across consisting of approximately 10m detectors including mosaics of different frequencies and probably low-light-level TV, phased array radar and laser radar. The infra-red sensors will incorporate integral data processing, thus obviating much of the need for complex linking to a central computer. To put HALO into orbit will require some six space shuttle loads of equipment and the whole system cannot be achieved without the shuttle. Supposedly on schedule for the 1990s, HALO will track ballistic missiles, bombers and cruise missiles and detect, classify and track satellites, using its mass of sensors tuned to a variety of wavelengths, depending on the target to be surveyed. Although HALO is not a weapon, its installation in space will still violate the **ABM** Treaty; its sensors are not radar and they are not based on the ground.

See also **NORAD**

hard bases, silos and similar missile installations or military command posts which have extra protection, usually in the form of reinforced concrete defences and the construction of subterranean bunkers, against incoming nuclear weapons. Such hardening must be reinforced to keep pace with advances in the strength and accuracy of new weapons and it is generally accepted that if the hardened silo is to be anything but a static concrete shroud rather than a useful asset to a weapons system, it cannot realistically be expected to survive a direct hit. Minuteman silos are hardened to withstand a pressure of 2,500 pounds per square inch (psi); a brick house explodes under 5–10 psi. Two-on-one **cross-targeting** is assumed to guarantee the destruction of all hardened targets today. The main hardened command posts in the US are the **NORAD** headquarters in Colorado, the **SAC** headquarters at Offutt Air Force Base, the National Military Command Centre (**NMCC**) in the Pentagon and the Alternative NMCC near Fort Richie, Maryland. Since all these posts are accepted as being expendable once hostilities begin, the US command will as soon as possible be transferred to the flying command post – the **kneecap** – which it is hoped will survive the attack.

hard target kill potential the extent to which an **ICBM** can be assumed to destroy a target that has been specifically protected against its war-heads. It has been accepted that ICBMs have this capability, but the introduction of the **Trident** II D5 missile (**SLBM**) will extend this threat to submarine-launched missiles, hitherto considered only capable of destroying soft targets.
See also **MARV**

hardware the military *materiel* possessed by a given state or military force. In this context, in an extension of the usual computer terminology, the 'software' is the personnel who use and operate the machinery and weapons.

H

hawk an advocate of an aggressive posture and policy in foreign relations. Coined in 1798 as 'war hawks' by Thomas Jefferson to describe those who wanted a war with France and later extended to those who, in 1812, actually achieved a war with England. Hawk enjoyed a popular revival during the Vietnam War, drawing direct inspiration from a Stewart Alsop/Charles Bartlett article – which also spread the political use of **dove** – following the Cuban Missile Crisis of 1962.
See also **dove**

high end of the conflict spectrum a euphemism delivered by US National Security Advisor William Clark, 1982. War.

High Frontier a system of space-based anti-ballistic missile defences originated by a private study, backed by right-wing funding, and fronted by Lieutenant-General Daniel O. Graham, former director of the Defense Intelligence Agency. Graham had previously been associated with a similar study by the right-wing Heritage Foundation, some of whose leading members are also close advisers of President Reagan, but after falling out over details of installing the system with his fellow expert nuclear scientist Edward Teller, Graham instituted his own $500,000 study. Delivered in mid-1982 after eighteen months gestation, High Frontier essentially suggested the building up of a space defence system based on existing technology. This would meet what Graham felt was an urgent need (a contrary view to Teller, who proposed waiting for the development of suitable technology prior to building such a system). High Frontier proposed a three-tiered system of defence. The first layer, using existing technology, would consist of 432 US satellites armed with non-nuclear missiles, including chemical lasers, intended to intercept Soviet missiles in their first, boost phase of flight. A second layer of non-nuclear missiles would act as **ABMs** surrounding US **ICBM** sites from those missiles that were still functioning. Once these initial tiers were in place, a further layer, added four or five years later, would utilise particle-beam weapons (**PBW**) and similar arcane systems. High Frontier, Graham promised, would replace **assured destruction** with assured survival (**MAS**). The Pentagon reviewed the study, finding against it in November 1982, citing the lack of suitable technology as the basis for rejection. A panel analysing space weapons for the Congressional Office of Technology backed up the Pentagon; High Frontier was 'a defensive system of extremely limited capability' or, as Edward Teller had put it, while the system might cost a hundred billion dollars, 'the Soviets can get rid of (it) for ten billion'. Despite this rejection, the President himself was impressed. Prior to his 'Star Wars' speech (**SDI**) of March 1983, he referred to the study often and it undoubtedly influenced that defence initiative. In 1984 Graham organised the American Space War Committee, designed to drum up support for the SDI and to collect funds for the backing of pro space defence candidates to Congress. The Committee concentrates on the defeat of incumbent Congressmen who oppose the SDI programme.

See also **BMD, SDI, star wars**

HIT acronym for Homing Interceptor Technology. A direct-ascent anti-satellite interceptor warhead designed for the destruction of satellites by collision. These non-nuclear warheads are less than 12 inches long, 7 inches in diameter, and weigh about 14 lbs. They incorporate a long wavelength infra-red (LWIR) seeker to home in on their target, a guidance system, a device to hold them right-side up and solid propellant rocket motors for manoeuvring in space. The HIT vehicle will destroy its target when they meet at a relative speed of 27,000 mph. It will also dispense a 'screen' of metal rods to increase its kill radius. Variations on the basic HIT technology include a vehicle with an unfolding 'umbrella', which has metal slugs attached to its ribs, and one that spits out concentric circles of metal cubes, thus maximising its kill radius. Given that HIT qualifies as an area defence system, and as such contravenes the **ABM** Treaty, Congress has ordered its development to be halted. Despite this ban, the system is still being researched and developed. By the late 1980s the Pentagon hopes to have a HIT vehicle that can destroy surveillance satellites on geosynchronous orbits 23,000 miles above the earth.

See also **ASAT, LoADS**

HOE acronym for Homing Overlay Experiment. Part of experiments on 'layered' ballistic missile defence, dealing specifically with the exo-atmospheric stage of a missile's flight to its target, 300,000 feet and higher. A series of four tests, launched in 1982, from Kwajalein Atoll in the Pacific aims to develop a system that can destroy 96 per cent of incoming missiles before they re-enter the atmosphere, at which point they become the subject of 'terminal layer' defence. The intention of HOE is to deploy space-based mosaic infra-red sensors, possibly aided by a designating optical tracker (DOT) vehicle, which will isolate targets and then work out the precise intercept trajectory necessary for the missile to be destroyed. Interceptor missiles will be launched, using the **HIT** system to launch non-nuclear missiles on a collision course with the hostile weapons.

hold-up the total amount of material set aside in a separation plant for the manufacturing of nuclear warheads.

homebodies the nickname given by USAF long-range strategic bomber crews to the **CONUS**-based missile launch crews.

horizontal escalation a situation in which the response to one crisis is to initiate another one elsewhere.

See also **escalation**

horizontal proliferation an increase in the numbers of nations possessing nuclear weapons. Thus **vertical proliferation** – an increase in the arsenals of nuclear weapons held by the nuclear-capable nations. Under the terms of the Nuclear Non-Proliferation Treaty signed by 110 nations in 1968, the nuclear-capable nations undertook neither to give nuclear weapons nor promote the development of such weapons to any country that did not have this capability. The non-nuclear capable nations undertook neither to accept nuclear weapons nor to research into them. The signatories, however, did not include those nations (none of them superpowers) who were on the verge of becoming or actually were nuclear capable – Argentina, Brazil, India, Israel, Pakistan and South Africa.

hostility containment a state of military invulnerability that would guarantee the defeat of any aggressive action against the US. Devotees of space-based weaponry consider such arms to be the best way to achieve this 'full control of US destiny' and 'long-term security for the earth's population' (from pamphlet issued by Rockwell Rocketdyne).

hot line a telex link between the White House and the Kremlin designed for use during any international crisis and specifically during a potential escalation towards nuclear war. Established by President Kennedy and Premier Khruschev in the 'Hot Line' Agreement, 1963. The 'Hot Line Moderation' Agreement of 1971 added two additional circuits which use satellite communications systems. Current moves are aimed to update the hot line with modern computer technology, but this decision has not been finalised.

hotspotter those theorists of the results of a nuclear explosion who believe that the resultant radiation will accumulate in 'hot spots' – areas of concentrated radiation – rather than simply spreading throughout the entire contaminated area. The hot spots so created would be the sites of maximum biological damage to humans, flora and fauna.

See also **averager**

hot-turn for a military aircraft to return to base, refuel, rearm and take off on a new sortie without ever turning off its engines, which thus remain 'hot' during the 'turn'.

humint abbreviation for human intelligence. Intelligence gleaned from human agents, i.e. traditional spying.
See also **comint, elint, sigint, telint**

hypocentre the ground directly below the heart of a nuclear explosion. Originally the central point from which an earthquake spreads.
See also **ground zero**

I

ICBM acronym for inter-continental ballistic missile. A missile that is capable of penetrating targets in either the USA or the USSR after being fired from a site on the territory of the opposite superpower or from a strategic submarine. As defined by both sides in the **SALT II** talks: 'land based launchers of ballistic missiles capable of a range in excess of the shortest distance between the north-east border of the US and the north-west border of the continental part of the USSR, that is, a range in excess of 5,500 kilometres'. Essentially the ICBM is a small space rocket (and both sides use rockets that have also taken men into space) which comprises three stages – the booster for take-off, a post-boost vehicle (the **bus**) for the intercontinental journey, then a re-entry vehicle, with its warhead(s) and individual motor and guidance system(s) for the descent onto the target(s). Missile guidance is based on inertial navigation, combined with precision mapping techniques developed from satellite surveillance, and can guarantee accuracy of between 100 and 30 metres on target.

Both superpowers used their share of captured German rocket scientists to develop missile systems after World War II. The US 'Teapot Committee', established 1950, led to the deployment of the first US ICBM, based on liquid fuelled Atlas and Titan rockets, in 1958. The Russian SS-6, used to put Sputnik-1 into space, gave the Soviets a similar capability in 1957. Both sides kept up ICBM programmes. As of SALT II (1979) the US possessed 1,052 missiles, the Soviets 1,398 – both sides **MIRV**ing these weapons with multiple warheads since the mid-1960s. The basic US missile force, the second 'leg' of the **strategic triad** is made up of Titan II and Minuteman II and III missiles. The Titan, introduced in 1963, is 100 feet long, 10 feet at its widest point, flies at 15,000 mph with an 800-mile ceiling, and delivers a single 5 megaton warhead; there are three wings of eighteen Titan IIs each deployed in the US.

Minuteman II (more sophisticated successor to the Minuteman I, deployed in 1961) delivers a 2 megaton warhead after a 15,000 mph flight. Solid-fuelled, it has greater accuracy, range and payload than the Titan; 450 are currently in service. The main US missile is the Minuteman III (the LGM-30G), deployed in 1975; 60 feet long, 6 feet at its widest point, weighing 78,000 lb, it has an 8,000-mile range and delivers three MIRVed warheads of 170–220 KT of TNT each (some twelve to fourteen 'Hiroshimas') within a **CEP** of 1 nautical mile. The introduction since 1979 of the super-accurate Mk 12A warhead on 300 missiles has cut this down to 0.12 n.m. These warheads have an 88 per cent chance of crushing a silo hardened to 1,000 psi (the current average). There are 550 Minuteman IIIs in the US arsenal. US missile-related personnel include 2,400 launch crew plus 5,000 maintenance men. ICBMs, as the second leg of the triad – their annual cost is only a third of the **strategic submarine** and a quarter of the **SAC** bomber fleets – are relatively less vital to the US than the Strategic Rocket Forces, employing *c.* 378,000 personnel, are to the Soviets. The lack of **FBS** and the geography of the USSR means that in their triad the ICBM stands first. Thus the likelihood of mutual reduction in ICBM forces remains unlikely – they are by no means of equal importance. Based in twenty-eight sites (including two test sites) across the USSR are a variety of SS-11s, SS-16s, SS-17s, SS-18s and SS-19s. The SS-16 was ostensibly banned at SALT II, but experts believe that it may yet be deployed. The major Soviet missiles are the SS-18s, the largest ICBM deployed by either power. Some 308 of these, of which 250 are armed with ten 20 MT MIRVs, are currently in service. They have a range of up to 8,000 miles and a CEP of around 450 feet. Approximately 300 of the second-ranked missile, the SS-19 are deployed. They can deliver three 550 KT MIRVs over a range of 6,000 miles to a CEP of 1,000 feet. Despite their relative accuracy, neither the SS-18 nor SS-19 can rival Minuteman III for accuracy. Conversely, the Soviets have some 2,500 of such warheads, whereas the US has only 900.

US missiles are divided into traditional USAF 'wings'; each wing comprises three squadrons which in turn have five flights of ten launchers each. Given the vulnerability of static silos, each wing is dispersed over a wide area, the largest over 1,800 square miles. Individual silos, protected by wire fences and surrounded by ground-level sensors, are sited at least 3 miles apart. Silos are 75 feet deep, 12 feet wide, with equipment rooms buried at the base. The missile itself is protected by a steel and concrete shield weighing 100 tons. Launch control sites, at least 5 miles from their silos, are manned by two SAC officers – usually Captains or Lieutenants in their early twenties. On warning of an attack – an oscillating note on a loudspeaker – the crew shut the blastproof doors and turn on emergency air supplies. A printed code is transmitted through a telex and the speakers announce 'Gentlemen, you have received an authorised launch instruction from the National Command Authority.' The officers then use two keys to unlock a strongbox in which are 'authentification codes' to double-check the initial launch command. They then strap themselves into two chairs, at right angles and 12 feet apart. Setting their individual enabling codes, held in each man's memory, they arm the missiles. They then turn their keys in two locks labelled 'Off/Set/Launch' within two seconds of each other, holding them for five seconds against a spring at 'Launch'. When the 'Missile Away' light appears, their task is complete. For a successful launch a further pair of officers in another control post must simultaneously 'vote' for the launch to proceed. In case of malfunction and destruction, each control post can launch an entire squadron of missiles and any one post can override its fellow(s). Once the missiles are fired, there is no recall. Plans are developing for a fleet of EC-135C aircraft which will be able to monitor, control and retarget ICBMs from the air.

The vulnerability of the silo-based missiles in the face of ever-increasing ICBM accuracy led to the development of the **MX** missile, which would have a mobile launcher and thus vastly increased **survivability**. The massive costs of the MX, coupled with the inability to date of the Pentagon to settle on a suitable basing system (**dense pack, race track**) has meant that, in reality, the vulnerable Minuteman II and III remain the prime US missiles. Current compromise plans are to put the first MXs into existing silos, and work out the basing later. Parallel to MX development is a scheme for the regular Minuteman arsenal whereby missiles could be **launched on warning** (LOW), then 'parked' in space, similarly to a bomber's

fail-safe position, and only activated into the programmed on-target flight when that attack was verified. What would happen were the attack to be proved illusory has not been stated.

See also **SLBM**

IFF acronym for identification friend or foe. Aircraft transponder for air-to-air or air-to-ground communications.

improved war outcome the strategic aim of limiting war damage to the population and resources of one's own nation and its allies, and of improving, if possible, the military-political outcome of a war. Such a war would entail a **counterforce** rather than **countervalue** strategy.

See also **damage limitation**

INF talks acronym for Intermediate-range Nuclear Forces Talks. By the late 1970s the US was planning to deploy a new generation of medium-range missiles in Europe to maintain the nuclear umbrella over the NATO allies. To this end, the Tomahawk **cruise missile** – in ground- and air-launched versions – and the US Army's Pershing II missile were scheduled for deployment in late 1983. While the allies wished to see this carried out, there had been developed the **dual-track** policy in 1979; weapons should be deployed for the defence of their territories, but simultaneously there should be negotiations with Russia in the hope of arms control, even when including the limiting of such weapons. In October 1980 President Carter duly sent a team to Geneva to pursue this negotiating 'track'. The meetings were soon negated by Carter's electoral defeat but some 'markers' were laid down for future talks; in essence the goal was equality in Euro-strategic weapons. The US wanted the Soviet's **MIRV**ed SS-20s reduced, while the Russians wished to have the deployment of cruise and Pershing II cancelled. The new Reagan Administration, broadly hostile to any legacy of the Carter era, had no great commitment to dual-track, but pursued it to appease the allies, who were hinting that deployment might not be so simple if talks were not re-started in Geneva. In May 1981 Reagan announced a decision 'to begin negotiations with the Soviet Union (on European nuclear forces) within the **SALT** framework by the end of the year'. For policy, Reagan chose the **zero option**, first advocated by Germany's Helmut Schmidt in 1980, whereby were the Soviets to remove their own medium-range missiles – the SS-4, SS-5 and in particular the new SS-20 – then there would be no need for the US to deploy cruise or Pershing II. Initially rejected in Washington as a pacifists' charter, zero option became essential to the INF talks. From the very outset many factors combined to bedevil the talks. Inevitably both sides saw Europe in completely opposite ways. Where Soviet mathematics saw equality, US totals gave Russia a 6:1 advantage. With zero option, the Russians saw a US advantage of 2:1. The Russians wished to include French and UK forces as well as carrier-based aircraft. The US sought to reduce Soviet missile bases in the Far East as well as in Europe. Even the name of the talks was unsettled when they commenced in 1981: originally the 'Theatre Nuclear Forces Talks', this term seemed to Europeans to hint at the **decoupling** of their own and US forces; 'Intermediate-range' implied that these weapons were simply another part of the overall US–NATO arsenal; the Russians wished to reject TNF and INF, demanding the inclusion of 'medium range systems in Europe' in the title; the US rejected any mention of Europe. The title remained unresolved throughout.

The negotiations stayed relatively sober, with a minimum of polemic – other than Reagan's periodic outbursts for home consumption – on either side. Instead the numbers were constantly rejigged in a series of attempts to progress which soon bogged down in stalemate. Perhaps the nearest moment to a breakthrough came in the ultra-private 'walk in the woods' taken on 16 July 1982 by Paul Nitze for the US and Yuli Kvitsinsky for Russia. The compromise they developed might have led to a treaty but their masters in Washington and Moscow rejected the package, a major feature of which had been the cancellation of Pershing, termed by a Washington hardliner as 'an act of intellectual and political cowardice'. Once the 'walk in the woods' had failed, the INF talks moved steadily to collapse. Propaganda took over from constructive discussion. The Soviets began to threaten a walk-out were cruise and Pershing II deployed on schedule. The shooting down of the Korean airliner in September 1983 destroyed what was left of the talks. Unprecedented personal acrimony soured relations in Geneva, and international abuse intensified the problems. In November 1983 the first Tomahawks arrived in England, the first Pershings in West Germany. On 23 November, the day the Pershings went on station in Mutlangen, the Soviets carried out their threat and walked out of the INF talks.

Like the **START** talks, which ran a parallel course, the INF negotiations never had much chance. Rival obsessions, rival interpretations of the *status quo*, rival fears of the opposite number, all combined to undermine the slim chance of an effective compromise. The Soviets as ever depended on US initiatives on which they would base their counter-initiative. US moves were confounded by three problems: the basic distrust shown by the administration towards their supposed European allies; a willingness to let themselves be side-tracked by minor detail instead of promoting major policy; an absolute refusal to alter the pre-set deployment schedules for the new weapons systems, even if such postponement might have resulted in a treaty. The propensity of the President to relate nuclear talks to those he had carried out for the Screen Actors' Guild thirty years previously hardly helped a difficult situation. By 1985 the new systems were in place, as were the Soviet SS-20s. It does not appear that either side is seriously interested in altering that position.

I

initial boost phase the period of a missile's flight that follows immediately on its launch: during this period the infra-red emanations from the heat of its rocket engine are vulnerable to surveillance by scanning systems and thus the rockets can themselves be targeted by anti-missile defences triggered by these scanners.

integrated battlefield a battlefield on which any combination of conventional, nuclear, chemical and biological weapons are used.

See also **ABC warfare, CW, NBC warfare**

intervention area the defined limit of operations in a small, supposedly controlled war.

See also **austere wars, escalation control**

intra-war period (*or* trans-SIOP period) the period during which the actual nuclear exchanges are taking place and the **SIOP** is actually being put into practice.

See also **SIOP**

IONDS acronym for Integrated Operational Nuclear Detection System. A system carried on board the **Vela** satellite to an altitude of 70,000 miles and used to detect atmospheric nuclear tests. When installed on the proposed **NAVSTAR** navigational satellites, IONDS will be integrated with the **C^3I** network to check damage sustained by both the US and the USSR during/after a nuclear attack.

See also **damage assessment, NUDETS**

iron

(1) all magnetic parts of an aircraft's construction, irrespective of the actual metal involved.

(2) any bomb that has no guidance system and is simply dropped vertically onto the target below.

See also **smart bomb**

I

J

JEEP acronym for Joint Emergency Evacuation Plan. The contingency plans for the evacuation of key personnel from Washington in the event of a nuclear attack. Army and Air Force helicopters take the first forty-four of 243 selected personnel – elite scientists, officials, technicians, all holding a JEEP-1 identification – to the Alternate National Military Command Centre ('Site R') at Raven Rock and to the civilian government emergency bunker, 'The Special Facility', in Mt Weather, northern Virginia. All these people have been chosen to run the country during and after a war; in peacetime they remain on permanent standby.

Joe I the first testing by the Soviets of an atomic weapon in August 1949. Named for the then Russian leader, 'Uncle Joe' Stalin.

K

Kahn energy the quantity of fission energy required for the destruction of one major nation's total population, assuming the absence of any adequate civil defence plans or of shelters. For either the US or the USSR this has been estimated at 10,000,000,000 tons of TNT. Named after Herman Kahn (born 1922), the nuclear futurologist and author of *Thinking About the Unthinkable* (1962), *On Escalation* (1965), etc.

Kneecap (*or* NEACP) acronym for the National Emergency Airborne Command Post. A converted Boeing 707 that will be used as an alternative Presidential command post in the event of a nuclear war. It is assumed by the Pentagon that in the event of a nuclear war none of the ground-based command posts, all of which will be priority targets for Soviet missiles, will survive a first strike. The President, plus the Secretary of Defense and the Joint Chiefs of Staff, will therefore take a seven-minute helicopter ride to Andrews Air Force Base and take off in the Kneecap. From here the nuclear exchanges can be carried out and the **SIOP** executed. The 707, which will thus be the central pivot of all US **C^{3}I**, can stay in the air for ten hours before taking on midair refuelling and is equipped with computers, duplicate **go-codes** and other command needs; aside from the President and his advisers it carries fifteen staff officers and twenty-seven crew. It is believed that the Kneecap will survive by virtue of its flying above the conflagration, but there is no guarantee that it will prove impervious to the massive dust storms that nuclear bombs release into the atmosphere. A commercial version of the 707 has been recorded as losing engine power when passing through high-altitude dust from a volcanic eruption.

See also **Looking Glass, WWMCCS**

L

lampshade abbreviation for radiation lampshade. A device for determining the height of an atomic **air burst**; it is about 1 foot wide and shaped like a lampshade.

latent period the time that elapses between the exposure of an individual to radioactive **fallout** and the onset of the fatal effects of that fallout.

launch on warning (LOW) the firing of one's own missiles on hearing that enemy missiles have been fired but have not yet arrived on target. The intention is to evacuate silos that have doubtless been targeted and which, with current **ICBM** accuracy, are unlikely, even when hardened, to withstand a direct hit. While LOW obviously increases the speed of US response to a hostile attack, its dependence on computerised sensors and early-warning systems can only mean that there exists a dangerous potential of a war launched through a computer malfunction. Given that the **NORAD** computer has on several occasions sensed an incoming strike on the instructions of a malfunctioning microchip, this problem remains a constant threat to world peace.

See also **attack options**

LD-50 abbreviation for lethal dose for 50 per cent. The dose of radiation required to kill 50 per cent of a given population within a specified time.

leakage the penetration of all lines and methods of defence and the successful impacting on target of a missile. A current assessment shows that it requires only 5 per cent of the total USSR missile arsenal to leak through any feasible US defences for the destruction of 50 per cent of the US population.

lethality the ability of a weapon and the technology of its launch platform to locate, hit and destroy targets. The formula for calculating lethality declares that lethality is directly proportional to the two-thirds power of the warhead explosive yield (megaton equivalent) and inversely proportional to the accuracy (**CEP**) squared.

linkage the linking within superpower relations, especially in the field of arms negotiations, of progress in military and diplomatic accords with that in 'humanitarian' and social issues, especially as regards Soviet interests in the Third World. Particularly espoused by the Carter Administration (1976–80) during which Congress refused to ratify **SALT II** until Russia showed itself willing to take real steps to improve domestic policies on dissidents and 'human rights', to set up a grain deal with the US, to moderate 'imperialistic' ambitions in Africa, etc. Linkage alters as to the chronology; US negotiations have variously cited Soviet activities in Poland, Afghanistan and (by Cuban proxy) Angola as well as the shooting down (in 1983) of Korean Airlines flight KE007 as pertinent to progress in contemporary talks. Whether this 'humanitarian' version of diplomatic blackmail actually works is debatable. The Soviets do not seem particularly impressed, knowing that policies are made for less idealistic reasons; similarly, many members of the US government are far more influenced by the harsher demands of international realpolitik than by linkage.

See also ***détente***

Little Boy the first atomic bomb, dropped on Hiroshima at 8.15 am on 6 August 1945. The bomb, 3 metres long, weighing 4,000 kilograms, was exploded in an **air burst** 510 metres above the city, with an explosive yield of a minimum of 12,000 tons (12 KT) of TNT.

LoADS acronym for Low-Altitude Defence System. A ballistic missile defence system designed specifically to eliminate those 4 per cent of hostile missiles that can be presumed to elude all **BMD** systems that would be targeted on incoming missiles and presumably successful in destroying them at earlier stages of their flight. Ground-based radars would calculate the intercept trajectory and the missiles would be attacked by a gun-launched hypervelocity interceptor. LoADS would destroy missiles below 50,000 feet – possibly as low as 6,000–8,000 feet – with its own small nuclear bombs of *c.* 2 KT yield. The interceptor would be very manoeuvrable, guided by a millimetre-wave radar seeker to home in on its target. Such **penaids** as the Soviets are known to use would have burnt up in the atmosphere and the real target would be vulnerable. LoADS is limited only by the time factor involved: the interceptor must be launched within ten seconds of sighting the warhead; anything over fifteen seconds fails to pre-empt the hostile explosion.

See also **HIT**

look-down shoot-down capability an airborne radar system, under development by the Soviets as a counter to the US *AWACS*, particularly geared to spotting aircraft and **cruise missiles** attempting to elude conventional ground-based radar observation nets. The result of such a capability might well negate the usefulness of cruise and as such render any use of these missiles as a positive bargaining chip pointless.

Looking Glass the flying command post which preceded **Cover All**; so called because its capabilities reflected (as a mirror) in the air the same command and control functions as existed at land-based command posts.

Loran-C abbreviation for long range navigation. The use of radio signals from special ground stations for military (and civilian) navigation. The Loran-C system provides pulsing low frequency (LF) signals that can penetrate 9–12 feet of water and sends very slow – fifty letters/minute – messages. Obviously such stations can only be based in friendly countries, and thus loran systems have strictly definable geographical limits.

L

LOW acronym for **launch on warning**.

lucrative target any target considered worthy of destruction.

M

MAD
See **assured destruction**

madman theory according to his former aide H. R. Haldeman, a theory developed by President Nixon whereby an implied threat of nuclear immolation would bring the N. Vietnamese to the conference table. To quote Haldeman's memoirs *The Ends of Power* (1978) Nixon explained 'I want the North Vietnamese to believe I've reached the point where I might do *anything* to stop the war. We'll just slip the word to them that "for God's sake, you know Nixon is obsessed about Communism. We can't restrain him when he's angry – and he has his hand on the *nuclear button*!" – and Ho Chi Minh himself will be in Paris in two days begging for peace.'

MAP acronym for Multiple Aim Point system. One of the systems proposed for the protection of the **MX** missile. A concept whereby the vulnerability of a static silo-based missile can be reduced by shuttling it around between a variety of identical underground silos; such shuttling would theoretically confuse hostile targeting.
See also **dense pack, race track**

MARV acronym for manoeuvrable re-entry vehicle. Any missile of which the warhead can be steered electronically, usually by internal inertial navigation guidance systems. The original MARV was named the Special Re-entry Body (SRB) and was equipped with an aerodynamic design which enabled it to fly like an aircraft on entering the atmosphere. MARVed weapons can rely on mid-course and terminal guidance options that include television, imaging infra-red laser and distance-measuring equipment (DME). Such weapons are also able to take evasive action if targeted by another missile. MARVing has added appreciably to the accuracy of **MIRV**ed missiles, which would otherwise be susceptible to atmospheric conditions and other random phenomena on re-entry into the atmosphere. Integrated with the highly accurate **NAVSTAR** global positioning guidance system, an advanced version of the MARV is possibly scheduled for use on the **Trident** II **SLBM** and could give it an accuracy on target of only 30 feet. The potential of MARVed weapons is massive: with Trident II missiles, each carrying seventeen 75 KT MARVed warheads, it would require only seven US submarines to destroy all but 140 of the Soviet's 1,398 land-based **ICBM**s; a second wave, requiring one more submarine, would leave just fourteen silos intact.

See also **ASMS, smart bomb**

MAS acronym for mutually assured survival. Coined by Max M. Kampelman, a leading negotiator in the 1985 arms control talks in Geneva; the favoured gospel of the originators of the **High Frontier** study, the foremost supporters of **Star Wars** development. While deterrence by **MAD** is 'a time worn and morally bankrupt doctrine' (Gen. Daniel O. Graham, *New York Review of Books* 11 April 1985), the **SDI**, with its space-based super-defences, would ensure that under the stern but necessary umbrella of US omnipotence, neither side would need to launch an attack – thus both would be assured survival; a survival, of course, that could only be guaranteed in this extreme example of the Orwellian 'war is peace' philosophy.

massive retaliation (*or* optimum mix) the US nuclear policy as put forward during the Eisenhower administration. The concept that, since the US possessed overwhelming superiority in the arms race, the Soviet should appreciate that whatever military schemes they envisaged, great or small, localised or intercontinental, the US strategic bomber fleet would obliterate their country with nuclear weapons. Europe itself was considered immune from attack after its arming with a variety of speedily developed tactical nuclear weapons in the late 1950s. Such vaunted invincibility began to falter by 1957 when the Soviets produced the SS-6 rocket, capable both of sending Sputnik-1 into space and delivering a warhead launched in Arctic Russia onto any desired target in **CONUS**. By 1960, and the election of President Kennedy, massive retaliation was a dead duck; a new **SIOP** was worked out and US nuclear policy turned to **counterforce** targeting and later **MAD**.

MBFR talks acronym for Mutual and Balanced Force Reduction talks. Begun in Vienna in 1973, these talks aimed to set up controls for non-nuclear forces based in Europe. Direct participants are the Benelux countries, W. Germany, the UK and the US; Czechoslovakia, E. Germany, Poland and the USSR. While both sides of negotiators have put forward a massive variety of possible ways of re-structuring the balance of forces, none has yet appeared realistic to each party. The talks were suspended shortly after the Russian walkout from the nuclear **START** and **INF** talks in January 1984.

MEECN acronym for Minimum Essential Emergency Communications Network. The network of communications systems – carried by airborne command posts, six VLF Navy transmitters sited around the globe from Maine to Australia, and two satellites – which have been reserved by the US military to ensure that a nuclear war would be carried on even after ground-based installations had been destroyed in a **first strike**. Especially powerful are the two satellites, first launched in 1976 and running a near-synchronous orbit several thousand miles apart; they can cover more than three-quarters of the earth's surface at one time, receiving communications from a circle on earth with a diameter of 8,000 miles. They have also been designed to withstand the effects of nuclear explosions by using miniature generators rather than solar cells. For all this technology, MEECN still fails in the area of submarine communications. These are subject to the poor qualities of water as a transmitter; popular schemes to overcome this drawback are in developing **Loran** and **ELF** wavelengths.

See also **Cover All, Looking Glass, NMCC, TACAMO**

megadeath 1,000,000 deaths. The basic unit for the large-scale assessment of casualties in a nuclear war. Thus: megacorpse, the detritus of a single megadeath; megadestruction, destruction caused alongside a number of megadeaths.

See also **acceptable casualties**

MHIV acronym for Miniature Homing Intercept Vehicle. The destructive payload of the US **PMALS ASAT** system designed to ram a target satellite at high speed and destroy it conclusively as its own 7,200 mph smashes into a target travelling at 10,000 mph. MHIV is a cylinder 12×13 inches filled with a variety of hi-tech instruments. Central to its operation are eight small telescopes which detect infra-red emissions from the target vehicle. These sensors are cooled to an extremely low temperature to capture this very faint light. Once the target has been sighted, the MHIV is moved towards it by fifty-six small rocket tubes which form the outer shell of the cylinder and which release their exhausts at right angles to the line of travel, from a ring of fifty-six holes sited around the centre of the vehicle. The MHIV is guided accurately into the path of the satellite by a ring-laser-gyro which governs the firing of the rockets and keeps the MHIV spinning at twenty times a second.

See also **ASAT, PMALS**

MIDAS acronym for Missile Detection Alarm System. An initially top secret military satellite programme initiated in the late 1950s. It was intended to detect missile launches recognising the infra-red emissions from the heat of the missile's rocket engines. The first MIDAS satellites were tested in 1960, and development was hurried after a U-2 spy plane was shot down over Russia, effectively ending spy plane flights, but the programme only became operational in 1972. As the programme developed, MIDAS was renamed Programme 461, then Programme 226, then Programme 949 and finally Programme 647L. These in turn became the nominally declassified Defence Support Programme, but its details are generally restricted. The DSP consists of three satellites held in geosynchronous orbit (locked in place 22,000 miles above the equator, moving at the same speed as the earth turns), one over S. America, one over the Indian Ocean and one over the central Pacific. From these vantage points their 12 feet long infra-red-sensitive telescopes, offset 7.5° from the body of the satellite, keep a constant surveillance over Russia, China and the oceans as it spins at five to seven revolutions a minute. MIDAS/DSP can pick up an **ICBM** launch within one minute of ignition, assuming the launch site is not obscured by cloud. The information is relayed to two secret readout stations at

Buckley Air National Guard Base, Aurora, Colo., and Pine Gap, near Alice Springs, Australia and from there to **SAC** headquarters, **NORAD**, the National and Alternate National Military Command Centres (**NMCC**). The most up-to-date DSP satellites have increased their original 2,000 detector cells to 80,000 – with a corresponding upgrade in precision. Measures have been included to defend them from possible Soviet laser attacks, and to harden them against high-level nuclear explosions. In pursuit of overall **survivability** the satellites will be able to perform far more of the data processing that was previously confined to the ground stations; since such stations are presumed to be eliminated in a first or retaliatory strike, the DSP satellites will be able to function autonomously and help keep alive US **C³I**.

Midgetman the growing disenchantment by 1982 with **MIRV**ed weapons, and the apparent inability of the Pentagon to decide once and for all on a basing system for the **MX**, led some US strategists to turn to a new weapons system – a small, single-warhead, mobile missile which, theoretically, should neither threaten nor provoke a **first strike**. Such missiles had been termed by negotiator Paul Nitze the 'little guys' (as opposed to Titan and Minuteman) and became generally known as Midgetman. Unlike those **ICBM**s currently in position, Midgetman would eschew hardened silos and move around the country as and when required. While this would dispense with the threat of Soviet missile accuracy, such deployment, with the same result as the MX's abortive closely spaced basing (**CSB**), would threaten to bring down a widespread barrage of relatively random but extremely powerful Soviet warheads. The announcement of Midgetman also had the predictable effect on Russian weaponeers; a parallel missile, initially called the PL-5, then SS-X-25, commenced testing. Midgetmanski, as NSC chairman Robert McFarlane named it, offered similar attributes to its US counterpart but boasted one important extra – it existed. While Midgetman remained subject to governmental debate, the SS-X-25 was undergoing tests. Initially the US attempted to link the missile with the SS-16, a discarded prototype of mobile missile, the further development of which was banned under **SALT II**, but such accusations were rebuffed – the missile was apparently an extension of the permissible SS-14. Inevitably, this disparity in progress meant that the Pentagon immediately claimed a 'mobility gap'. And while one senior aide to the Joint Chiefs of Staff condemned it as a mere fad – 'the strategic equivalent of the Hula Hoop' – the Reagan Administration was less sanguine. $600m was allocated to further development of Midgetman and other possible **SICBM**s in the 1984 budget. Although constructors Boeing and Martin Marietta were still fighting for the final contract in 1985, it was assumed that the system should be operational by 1990. Boeing suggested a three-stage solid fuel missile weighing 14 tons at launch, putting a **throw-weight** of 1,000 lb into a **CEP** of 300–500 feet. Martin Marietta proposed a modified Pershing II, with similar throw-weight and CEP as the Boeing version. Both systems would be deployed by road, using vehicles with low profiles and ground anchor systems which will harden them to resist up to 25 psi **overpressure**.

See also **SICBM**

MILSTAR acronym for Military Strategic-Tactical and Relay. A satellite system under development in 1985, designed to maximise communications technology in one vehicle for inter-military use during a nuclear war. According to Major-General Gerald Hendricks of the USAF Space Division, MILSTAR is 'designed to be a war-fighting system' which will work 'during all levels of conflict, have worldwide two-way communications, and be survivable and enduring'. Despite the accepted high standards in these areas (except the vital **survivability** that is the current preoccupation of US war planners) of the USN **FLTSATCOM** system, it is assumed that the multi-billion dollar MILSTAR will replace it. Among the more theoretical uses planned for MILSTAR may be for it to have a number of identical 'silent' partners stored in high orbits. If the functioning MILSTAR is destroyed, one of them may be activated to take its place.

See also **AFSATCOM, FLTSATCOM**

M

minimum deterrence the smallest quantity of nuclear weapons required to assure a potential attacker that they will suffer unacceptable national damage in a **retaliatory strike**. Such a form of deterrence (in effect the policy of **assured destruction** cut back to the barest necessary arsenals) would dispense with all but the vital warheads, thus making obsolete any 'war-fighting' or 'limited' capabilities, especially the short-range 'battlefield' nuclear weapons. The numbers involved in minimum deterrence vary; an overall cutback of 50 per cent in the US arsenal seems generally acceptable, although a figure as low as 500 warheads has been suggested. Complete dependence on submarine-launched missiles has also been posited, with the destruction of nearly all silo-based and bomber-launched missiles. Backed by a number of former Vietnam-era hawks, minimum deterrence has yet to find support from an incumbent US administration, although President Carter flirted with the concept of an all-**SLBM** force. The fears of 'missile gaps', 'laser gaps' – however spurious – plus the entrenched desire of the military-industrial complex for self-aggrandisement will continue to outlaw this version of strategic policy.

See also **assured destruction, countervailing strategy, deterrence**

MIRV acronym for multiple independently targeted re-entry vehicle. Separate warheads (**passengers**) carried by the same launch vehicle (the **bus**) and delivered by computerised internal and stellar inertial guidance (SIG) to multiple targets over an area of up to 20,000 square miles. The MIRV system in the final stage of the missile has its own set of directional jets, like a space capsule, and can thus manoeuvre from target to target. Increased accuracy is obtained from **MARV**ed systems, which compensate for the atmospheric conditions that can make re-entry otherwise unpredictable. The earliest MIRV was created in 1964 for the Polaris A-3 SLBM; it delivered three 200 KT warheads at a range of 2,500 nautical miles. The first MIRVed **ICBM** was tested in 1968; three independently targeted warheads were placed on a Minuteman III, and in 1970 the Polaris C-3 **SLBM** offered a bus with up to fourteen 50 KT passengers. Today's Minuteman missiles still have three warheads, the majority delivering 335 KT per RV. The MIRV programme had commenced in 1962, when Robert MacNamara initiated a swing in weapons development, from quantity ('more bang for your bucks') to quality, and from massive rockets to smaller and more accurate ones, a movement that continues today. Ostensibly the new weapon was designed to destroy

Soviet **ABM** systems and demonstrate US technological superiority. Such advantages were short-lived; the ABM treaty of 1972 wiped out that justification for MIRVing and the Russians responded to US superiority by rushing through their own development of the system. Given the Soviet preference for monster rockets, e.g. the SS-18, with a potential of thirty warheads per launcher, the narrowing of the technological gap soon meant that the US considered itself inferior in the 'MIRV gap' and in the possession of nuclear **throw-weight** (the total weight that can be delivered by a missile after the last stage of the delivery rocket has separated). In fact Soviet throw-weight superiority is more than balanced by US technical sophistication, especially in electronic miniaturisation, but for US hawks, who seized any excuse for boosting the arms race, the superficial disparity was convenient. Research began in 1972 on the development of the **MX** ('missile experimental') which was to rival the Soviet SS-18 and SS-19 as to throw-weight, and offer the additional factor of manoeuvrability – a counter to the **window of vulnerability** as the hawks termed the purported Soviet threat to US ICBMs that accrued to their extra throw-weight. The **SALT I** interim treaty (1972) effectively ignored MIRVs, concentrating on launch vehicles (particularly in limiting the Russian 'heavy' ICBMs to 308) rather than the warheads they carried. **SALT II** limited MIRVed ICBMs to 820 (with a further 500 MIRVs available to other – submarine – launch systems). The larger Soviet rockets were individually restricted as to warheads; SS-18 to ten, SS-19 to six and SS-17 to four. None of these restrictions dealt adequately or honestly with MIRVing and, by the initiation of the **INF** and **START** talks, it was apparent that warheads as well as launchers had to be limited in future. Proponents of 'de-MIRVing' put forward a concept that returned to a pre-MIRV world in which all launchers had but one warhead. The price for this, they accepted, was de-limiting the number of launchers a country could hold. Military reality soon defeated de-MIRVing; the fine-tuning of technology could no more be discarded than could the nuclear technology itself. When the START talks foundered in December 1983, MIRVed arsenals remained at the SALT II levels and the alleged throw-weight disparity persisted. The new talks in 1985 concentrated on a new phenomenon, the

Strategic Defence Initiative ('**Star Wars**'); the role of MIRVs remains in abeyance.

See also **CEP, ICBM, MARV, throw-weight**

missile envelope that area of the sky that can be saturated by a salvo of hostile missiles and which therefore will inevitably prove fatal for any target airplanes.

missile gap in 1959 the Gaither Committee reported to President Eisenhower that the Soviets were capable of firing 100 **ICBMs** at **CONUS** targets; additional reports from intelligence agencies predicted that the Soviet capability would rise to 1,000–1,500 missiles within five years. Although it was soon proved – thanks to Eisenhower's ordering of an increase in U-2 spy plane flights – that the Soviet missile programme was targeted on Western Europe and not on the US missile silos, and that the missile gap was as illusory as the bomber gap of the early 1950s, presidential challenger John F. Kennedy made it a major plank in his campaign. The Soviets, he claimed, had invested heavily in nuclear development, moving ahead in the arms race while a lethargic Eisenhower had sat back and allowed them their way. The issue was palpably bogus but the US public, inured to a decade of US superiority, mixed with sporadic panics that justified increased arms budgets, believed the Kennedy line, as did the Pentagon, whose production of ICBMs accelerated. In 1961 the Polaris weapons system was deployed, while the Soviets did not possess a counterpart until 1969; in 1964 the US silos held 834 ICBMs, four years before Russia had a comparable force. The new president appreciated the facts, and discontinued the USAF B-70 supersonic bomber programme; he did not, however, curtail missile production. A further counter to the 'gap' was to base more missiles in US forward areas – NATO allies and US aircraft carriers. It was the Soviet attempt to create their own forward base on Cuba that led to the crisis of late 1962. And it was Khruschev's 'blink', when the superpowers stood head to head, that determined Russia never again to let the US gain ICBM ascendancy.

modesty shield a 140,000 lb reinforced steel shield designed to protect the transporters of the **MX** missile from hostile surveillance.

M

Moscow criterion the belief amongst UK strategic planners that any UK weapon should be able to attack Moscow. This belief influenced the decision in 1973 to adopt the **Chevaline** modification of the Polaris A-3 missile rather than opting to replace the Polaris by the Poseidon missile.

MRBM acronym for medium range ballistic missile. A group of land-based ballistic missiles with a range between 900 km and 2,400 km. The US deploys Pershing II and Tomahawk (**cruise**) and the USSR has the near-obsolete SS-4 and the new SS-20. The status of these medium-range missiles, designed essentially for the European theatre, remains central to inter-power arms talks. The short-lived **zero option** of November 1981 was a direct, if cynical, response to the growing animosity towards the proposed deployment of Pershing II and cruise. On the other side, the Soviets continue to suggest cutbacks or deployment freezes on MRBMs. As of mid-1985 all these plans have failed and the missiles are being deployed; approximately 235 SS-20s targeted on W. Europe and a proposed 380 Pershing IIs and 464 Tomahawks targeted on the East.

See also **INF talks, theatre armaments**

MRV acronym for multiple re-entry vehicle. One of a number of warheads which can be carried on a single booster rocket. Unlike the more sophisticated **MIRV**s and **MARV**s which have replaced them, these warheads simply boost the on-target **throw-weight** of a given booster; they cannot be independently guided to a variety of targets.

See also **MARV, MIRV**

multiple kill capability any weapons platform – ship, airplane, tank – which holds more than a single type of weapon; guns and bombs, bombs and missiles, a variety of missile types, etc.

multistable deterrence a three-way theory of nuclear stability: (1) the capability of devastating **retaliation** following a hostile **first strike**; (2) the holding by both sides of so credible a first strike capability that neither would benefit from starting a war; (3) the **balance of terror** epitomised by (2) should lead to the reduction of potential tension flashpoints across the world.

muncher a Nimrod submarine reconnaissance aircraft, used by the RAF to track hostile submarines. The equivalent of the US **AWACS**, so-called from the supposedly lavish meals the Nimrod crews take on their 10-hour flights.

See also **AWACS**

MX acronym for Missile Experimental, Missile-X. Like its submarine-borne **SLBM** counterpart, the **Trident** missile, MX evolved from the **Strat-X** study of 1967, which launched the current US drive for strategic modernisation, or the creation of new and technologically sophisticated weapons systems. The inevitable ageing of the Titan and Minuteman III **ICBM** arsenals, plus the advances in missile accuracy that threatened their once-invulnerable hardened silos, made for the development of a missile that incorporated a mobile launcher. The MX is a four-stage ICBM, combining three stages of solid and one of liquid fuel. It is 72 feet long, 92 inches in diameter, with a weight of 190,000 lb (7.5 tons, three times heavier than the Minuteman III). It will use the highly accurate Advanced Inertial Reference Sphere (AIRS) guidance system to deliver ten **MIRV**s, each armed with the 300 KT Mk 21 warhead, at a minimum range of 7,000 nautical miles. AIRS will guarantee a basic **CEP** of 400–600 feet; using the **NAVSTAR** global positioning system, this can be reduced to 300 feet; adding **MARV** technology cuts it to 100 feet. MX has been designed to combine two important factors necessary in an ICBM: pinpoint accuracy on target; and, when a suitable basing system is developed, **survivability**. Ostensibly a **second-strike counterforce** weapon which will ride out a hostile attack, then act as the spearhead of a counter-attack, its very accuracy makes critics on both sides of the Iron Curtain suspect it has greater potential as a **first-strike** weapon than as a retaliatory one. For experts in diplomacy this makes it a highly destabilising factor in international relations. Testifying to the Towne Committee on the MX in Spring 1981, Caspar Weinberger remarked 'We need the MX missile, please tell us where we should put it,' thus underlining the most urgent problem concerned with MX – where and how to base it. Since full development began in 1972, a number of plans have been created; none to date has proved satisfactory. They include the following. (1) Buried trench. One trench would be dug for each missile, some 13 miles long. It would be covered in keystones, capable of sustaining **overpressure** up to 200 psi, but easily raised for the firing of the missile. For the proposed fleet of 300 MXs, the tunnels would have required some 4,000-odd miles, a distance greater than the width of the US. (2) Hybrid trench. In an effort to save space, there would be one hardened section of trench, with twenty to twenty-nine unhardened spurs. The missile would 'hide' in any given spur, thus eluding Soviet surveillance. (3) Semi-hard shelters. A number of hardened concrete bunkers, many of them empty. The MX transporter-erector-launcher (TEL) hides in one bunker and defies Soviet satellites before emerging to fire its weapon. All these systems, which were relatively cheap and relied on proven technology, were dismissed in 1978 when a MIT survey revealed that hardening to 200–300 psi could no longer withstand the current accuracy of hostile ICBMs.

Two 'shell game' systems were evolved to replace the trenches. (4) **MAP**, which relied on vertical shelters, in one of which would be the actual missile. (5) **race track**, using a closed-loop system of roadways, each of which would shuttle a missile around. The premise of these combinations of dummy missiles, real missiles, filled and empty shelters, was to provoke the enemy into expending as many as possible of his ICBMs to destroy each single MX. Planners claimed that the MAP system could withstand a 20,000 ICBM attack and still leave half the MX force intact; that such an attack would leave little of the US but the MXs was simply ignored. A variety of other schemes were suggested for US ICBM mobile basing, aimed primarily at the Minuteman III, but presumably considered for MX. (6) Air mobility. One idea was to deliver the missile by parachute from the tail of a carrier plane; the other used a 'land and launch' technique in which the carrier plane landed, rolled out the MX and its launcher, fired the missile and flew away. (7) Underwater systems, using either canisters strapped to diesel-powered submarines, which would surface in shallow water to fire their weapon, or vertical floating capsules which would be dumped from ships prior to remote detonation.

In 1981 President Reagan threw out all the above ideas and demanded intense research into three areas: air mobility; deep underground mountain basing (DUMB, see **deep basing**); a ballistic missile defence (**BMD**) system to protect the MX. All three areas proved useless: air mobile launchers were too expensive; deep-basing too slow in reaction time and possibly weak in communication; the BMD could not be finished to match the deployment schedule of the missile. BMD also contravened the **ABM** Treaty of 1972, but this apparently bulked less than the time factor. For a while a new system, (8) **dense pack** or closely spaced basing, which depended on **fratricide** to confuse and destroy incoming missiles, was popular. This one vanished by 1983 after Congress refused to vote funds for a project that seemed, like many predecessors, merely to attract the maximum possible saturation attack onto the US. Ironically, for a weapon that was intended for mobility, the current basing plan is to put a reduced deployment of 100 MXs into Minuteman silos, a system that, after billions of dollars expended on an alternative base, is now deemed, at least temporarily, less vulnerable than had been formerly avowed.

See also **deep basing, dense pack, fratricide, race track**

N

NAVSTAR acronym for Navigation System using Timing and Ranging. A sophisticated, navigational system based on ultra-accurate time-clocks which will provide US forces with sophisticated global positioning from a network of eighteen (eventually twenty-four) satellites. As 'one of the most important and far-reaching programmes in the Department of Defense', it will facilitate blind bombing, route navigation, artillery ranging, troop movements and rendezvous and will have particular effect on missile delivery, giving navigational accuracy to a **CEP** of 300 feet, enhanced with **MARV**ing to only 30 feet. NAVSTAR research started in the Navy Research Laboratory's Timation programme of the mid-1960s. It is based on the principle that if the velocity of two points and the time needed for a radio signal to travel between them are known, the distance between them can be calculated and extremely accurate navigational fixes can therefore be taken. The essence of the system is a timer of as near perfect accuracy as possible. The NRL and, in parallel, the USAF worked for nearly a decade on putting such clocks into space until, in 1973, both projects were amalgamated in the NAVSTAR Global Positioning System. Since then a series of prototypes, development and recently production satellites have been put into space. A mix of rubidium vapour and caesium clocks (respectively ten and a hundred times as accurate as quartz) are installed in them; future plans will replace these with hydrogen maser clocks, although the weight of these still presents a problem. Once installed, the full system will comprise eighteen satellites (though twenty-four remains the original figure) in six planes of orbit with three 'spares' orbiting in reserve. Each 1,735 lb satellite will orbit the earth once every 12 hours at a height of 12,500 miles, broadcasting simultaneously on two jamming-resistant frequencies. The satellites are kept on accurate orbits by sending a timed and precisely located signal to an earth station; this signal is processed and the predicted locations of that satellite over the next 24 hours are uploaded into the satellite's memory. Some 27,000 users from all four US services will be able to lock onto the GPS, using the orbits of any four satellites to place themselves in a highly accurate three-dimensional map, which accords with that used by any other GPS receiver. The information they receive will provide all-weather positioning accurate to 33 feet in any direction, velocity within 0.55 ft/second, and time synchronisation to a fraction of a microsecond. The latest generation of NAVSTAR satellites will also be fitted with **NUDETS** (nuclear detection systems) sensors. While NAVSTAR has many conventional uses, its potential in missile targeting is immense. The system was mooted for installation on the **MX** missile, but the accuracy of the MX, plus the US fear that Soviet jamming might be able to invalidate GPS, has ruled this out. Tested on the **Trident** missiles, GPS has been very accurate. While the use of GPS receivers on missiles is obviously an advantage, there are no current plans to install them, although the option doubtless remains open. On a war-planning level, some US experts see GPS as a novel form of extra-military pressure; if it can be shown to the enemy that GPS will give absolute accuracy to any strike, the system can be used as a threat, with missiles poised for action, in the hope of a diplomatic solution.

See also **IONDS**

NBC Warfare acronym for nuclear, biological and chemical battlefield.

See also **ABC, CW, integrated battlefield**

neutron bomb

See **enhanced radiation weapon**

NIE acronym for National Intelligence Estimate. The regular CIA assessment of the current nuclear capability of the USSR and the future structure and development of its nuclear forces.

nightwatch codename for the National Emergency Airborne Command Post.

See also **Kneecap, Looking Glass**

N

NMCC acronym for National Military Command Centre. The 'War Room' of the Pentagon, one of the four US military command centres which comprise the US National Military Command System and which would conduct a nuclear war. The oldest of the NMCS posts, the NMCC was originally known as the 'Joint War Room Annexe' and was set up in 1959 after the panic engendered by the launch of Sputnik I. The NMCC is in immediate contact with the other three (**SAC** headquarters, **NORAD** and the Alternate NMCC near Fort Richie, Maryland), with the US President in the White House Situation Room (a windowless basement beneath the Oval Office) and with US military commanders throughout the world. NMCC exists to execute instructions from the National Command Authority – the President and the Secretary of Defense – through all necessary channels of command and control in the strategic and tactical forces. The NMCC leans heavily on surveillance, damage assessment and similar planning information relayed by the NORAD computers in Cheyenne Mountain, Colo. Although the NMCC is hardened against nuclear attack, it is assumed that given current ICBM accuracy, neither it, nor probably its alternate facility, would survive in a war. In this case, all responsibilities would devolve upon the **Kneecap**.
See also **WWMCCS**

NMCS acronym for National Military Command System. The command system of all US nuclear forces, established in the late 1950s to coordinate the previously disparate branches of US defence. The consolidation followed the US military reaction to the launch of Sputnik, the implication of which was that the Soviets had developed a rocket powerful enough to challenge US ICBM superiority. Initially, experts from the USAF, which maintained control of strategic defences, produced a list of 'L-systems': continental air defence (416L); traffic control and landing (413L); weather observation (433L); intelligence handling (438L); ballistic missile warning (474L); air communications (480L); and satellite surveillance (496L). All these systems, like those developed in a simpler era of bomber wings, fighter wings and their ancillaries, had developed quite independently. By 1959 the USAF had 'capped' them all into one organisation, the NMCS, responsible ultimately to the National Command Authority (the President and the Secretary of State) and charged with the task of waging America's putative nuclear war.

See also **NMCC, NORAD, SAC**

no-city strategy

See **counterforce**

nominal yield weapons any nuclear bomb with an explosive **yield** of approximately 20,000 tons of TNT.

Non-Proliferation Treaty signed in 1968 by the US, the USSR, the UK and an open-ended list of non-nuclear powers (by 1983 there were 117 of these), this treaty sought to restrict the further growth of national possession of nuclear arms. It has three major provisions. (1) The commitment by those states that already possess nuclear weapons not to make them available to any country that does not have them. (2) A pledge by the non-nuclear countries not to seek nuclear arsenals and to accept the regulations and monitoring of the International Atomic Energy Agency as regards their 'peaceful' use of nuclear power; in return the advanced nations promised to offer their nuclear reactor expertise to their poorer fellows. (3) An obligation on behalf of the nations with nuclear weapons to start serious talks on arms control and nuclear disarmament. For all its vaunted importance, the NPT lacked signatures from those vital countries – Israel, South Africa and India – whose own nuclear programmes were reaching completion, as well as those of the smaller nuclear powers – China and France – neither of which chose to sign.

See also **proliferation**

NORAD acronym for North American Aerospace Defense Command. Unlike the Soviets, who have deployed anti-missile defences as permitted by the **ABM** Treaty (1972), the US depends not on weapons but on an elaborate network of complementary and overlapping surveillance systems to warn of imminent nuclear attack. Buried one-third of a mile beneath the granite of Cheyenne Mt, Colorado, are fifteen reinforced steel structures, mounted on shock-absorbing helical springs: this is the headquarters of NORAD (opened in 1966), one of the three hardened US command posts (the others are **SAC** HQ at Offutt Air Force Base and the War Room in the Pentagon). Originally established in the 1950s to locate and intercept Soviet bomber strikes, NORAD today, plugged into nineteen radars and nine special telescopic cameras across the world, is simply charged with spotting the incoming missiles and reporting their launch, progress and supposed targets to the President, the Pentagon and SAC. The NORAD complex also includes the Aerospace Defense Command (ADCOM) which in turn controls the Space Defense Operations Centre (SPADOC).

The responsibilities and operations of NORAD are as follows. (1) ADCOM. Controls three early warning satellites in synchronous orbit over the equator. One over the Indian Ocean spots Soviet missile plumes within 90 seconds of launch; these would be the first warning to the US of a **first strike**. The other two, respectively over the Atlantic and Pacific Oceans, look out for **SLBM**s. The problem with these satellites is that, dependent on infra-red sensors, they lose the missile once it has passed beyond the **initial boost phase** and lost the tell-tale 'plume'. Scheduled for deployment in 1986 is TEAL RUBY, a satellite-carried surveillance system, in effect a super-telescope, designed to take worldwide measurements of the infra-red background and register both friendly and hostile aircraft and missile presence. (2) SPADOC. This nerve centre of all NORAD-controlled surveillance and weapons systems monitors every aspect of the network. Its Space Detection and Tracking Stations (SPADATS) process some 10,500 inputs per day from worldwise sensors that track every object in space, including satellites, rocket and allied debris and, in the event, hostile missiles. Such objects are estimated at approximately 10,000 by the end of 1985. The heart of the SPADATS system is the USAF's 'Spacetrack', with its pair of massive radars at Eglin Air Force Base, Fla., and Shemya Is. in the Aleutians. The system is also fed by the USN NAVSPASUR (tracking satellites across the southern states). (3) BMEWS. The Ballistic Missile Early Warning System is made up of three overlapping radar arcs based on Clear, Alaska, Thule, Greenland, and Fylingdales, Yorkshire. These scanners can track anything coming out of the European landmass at a range of 3,000 miles. Currently BMEWS is restricted to boost-phase surveillance, but substantial updating will remedy this deficiency. First missile impact prediction facilities and then improved detection and tracking radars will be added to the system. (4) PAVE PAWS. Two phased array radars sited in Otis Air National Guard Base, Massachusetts, and Beale Air Force Base, California, watch for **SLBMs**. They also help with space tracking. Two further sites are planned for Georgia and Texas. (5) PAR. A Perimeter Acquisition Radar, sited at the former **ABM** base in North Dakota, is used by the USAF for north-facing space tracking by phased array radars which can spot missiles coming over the Pole at a range of 4,600 km. (6) FPS-85. A phased array radar in Florida conducts general surveillance of the Caribbean area and searches for **FOBS** 'wrong way round' missile attacks coming up from the South. (7) SEEK FROST and SEEK IGLOO. The original **DEW** (Distant Early Warning) **line** and Pinetree line (guarding N. America and Canada from northern bomber, then missile, attacks) are being updated in the mid-1980s. Currently both lines can detect high-level flight at up to 40,000 ft and 200 miles away, but cannot detect low-flying objects. The two lines are to be replaced by the SEEK FROST system and the USAF base in Alaska by SEEK IGLOO. (8) In addition to these systems, NORAD takes reports from **AWACS**, the flying surveillance planes, from two **OTH-B** (over-the-horizon backscatter) radars in Maine and Washington State and from the ROCCs (Regional Operations Control Centres) which control some forty-six radars in Canada and the US and monitor the entire complex of civil and military air traffic over CONUS. And although NORAD is an advisory rather than an executive system, its commander has access to a fleet of 320 F-15 fighters to be used to defend against bomber or cruise missile assault.

For all its computerised satellite-sensitive complexity, NORAD is by no means perfect. Within eighteen months of the installation in September 1979 of new computers, replacing the defunct models of 1961, the new system registered 147 false alarms of hostile attack, four of which raised worldwide US troop alert status by one level. While backup systems, verifiable with all sensors in one minute, ensured that the US did not launch World War III 'by accident', the fear that another forty-seven cent microchip can go down (the cause of the most notorious alarm in November 1979) cannot be dismissed lightly. Finally, even Cheyenne Mt is not considered absolutely safe;

NORAD maintains an alternative Space Defense Centre at Eglin Air Force Base.

nucflash
(1) US Dept of Defense Accident Code. An accidental or unauthorised incident involving detonation of a nuclear warhead by US forces which could create the risk of war with the USSR.
(2) Any warning of a (still) unidentified flying object on missile early warning radar.

nuclear cinc Nuclear commander-in-chief. The overall C-in-C – the US President – plus C-in-Cs Atlantic, Pacific and Europe. All nuclear cincs work from an airborne command post which would be launched as soon as there was received a positive indication of incoming hostile missiles.
See also **Looking Glass, Kneecap, Nightwatch**

nuclear freeze a nuclear freeze does not seek to reduce weapons or to promote disarmament, but simply to ban any further production of weapons, either in their current forms or as new systems. A call for such a freeze was narrowly rejected by the US Congress in 1982, but the general concept, which will preserve the current approximate parity between the Soviet and American strategic triads, for all the asymmetry between them this accepts, remains popular among the doves in government, the administration and the US scientific community. A freeze would demand an end to the production of the fissionable material used in nuclear weapons and of the manufacture and testing of warheads, the production and deployment of missiles and the testing of any new strategic bombers. Since current arsenals would be maintained, vital materials, such as tritium, could be replaced before they decayed dangerously. Nuclear submarines could be replaced at the end of their generally accepted 30-year lifetime; the gyroscopes and electrical systems that are kept running in all missiles, ready for instant use, would also be replaceable.

nuclear threshold that moment in an escalating crisis when nuclear weapons are used for the first time. Taken from Herman Kahn's theories of escalation in which 'intense crises' (restricted to use, however widespread, of conventional weapons) pass through the 'no nuclear use threshold' to 'bizarre crises' (starting with local, exemplary nuclear strikes and moving ever upwards).

See also **escalation ladder**

nuclear umbrella the concept that US nuclear weapons are to be used in defence of Europe as well as of the continental US.

See also **coupling**

nuclear winter the concept, currently popular amongst nuclear theorists, that the result of a prolonged nuclear interchange would be the destruction of the climate as we know it. Instead, beneath perpetual clouds of radioactive debris, would be increasingly colder temperatures, ruining crops, human and animal life and condemning the survivors of the war to a minimal existence in an endless 'winter'. There would be required only a fraction of the world's strategic arsenal – some 500–2,000 of the estimated 18,000 strategic warheads (ignoring the threat posed by the additional 35,000 tactical and intermediate weapons) – to trigger a climatic catastrophe that would engulf the entire planet, extending beyond the territories of the protagonists to those of distant neutrals. As Professor Carl Sagan, one of those who first formulated the theory, states: 'Cold, dark, radioactivity, pyrotoxins and ultraviolet light following a nuclear war . . . would imperil every survivor on the planet.' Former **SAC** Commander Curtis LeMay's threat to 'bomb the Viet Cong back to the Stone Age' would finally come to pass. If this theory is correct, and the figures for an effective **first strike** – some 2,200–4,500 attacking warheads – remain as they are, then, as Sagan has put it, 'a major first strike may be an act of national suicide, even if no retaliation occurs'.

See also **greenhouse effect**

NUDETS acronym for nuclear detection system. A computerised analysis of the progress and results of a nuclear attack, counting the missiles, checking their launch sites (for re-targeting of friendly missiles in a retaliatory attack), registering impact and destruction, and assessing the overall position following the strike. This enables the President or surviving

N

authority to make – in theory – a suitable decision as to the next step in the conflict.

See also **AWDREY**

O

O

oil burner routes published trans-American air routes along which the armed forces are permitted to carry out low-level, high-speed training missions.
See also **olive branch routes**

olive branch routes low-level trans-American training routes flown by B-52 bombers. From the **SAC** motto 'Peace Is Our Profession'.
See also **oil burner routes**

on call target a specific nuclear target which will be attacked on a direct command rather than simply at a certain time.

open skies policy proposed by President Eisenhower at the Geneva Summit Conference of 21 June 1955. A scheme whereby the superpowers would exchange military blueprints and allow aircraft flights over each other's territory. Given that the US then possessed a 5:1 superiority in nuclear warheads, the Russians rejected the policy out of hand. Despite this, the US commenced a programme of secret spying overflights by U-2 aircraft, a clandestine practice that collapsed after the plane piloted by Gary Powers was shot down in 1960, concomitantly wrecking the current summit talks. The State Department, with remarkable arrogance, then declared that, had the Russians accepted 'open skies', the flights would never have been necessary!

optimum mix
See **massive retaliation**

orange forces the 'hostile' force during NATO exercises and simulated wargames.
See also **blue forces**

OTH radar, OTH-B radar acronyms for over-the horizon radar and over-the-horizon backscatter radar. Radar that can transmit signals from objects that are out of the line of sight by following the earth's curvature, a facility denied normal radar scanners. OTH radar sends signals that hit the target then bounce up to the ionosphere before returning to the monitor; 'backscatter' means that the signals come back to the scanner along the same outgoing track. OTH radars have been established on the east and west coasts of the US, tracking incoming bombers or cruise missiles at a range of up to 1,800 miles.

See also **NORAD**

overkill the concept of being able to destroy a nuclear target more than once. Such a requirement justifies the building of massive arsenals and the theoretical launching of a massive strike, but has no useful military application.

overpressure nuclear blasts that are strong enough to destroy hardened silos or command bunkers; the amount of pressure generated by a nuclear explosion that exceeds the normal atmospheric pressure of 14.7 psi. Buildings collapse at 6 psi overpressure; humans can withstand levels up to 30 psi, but anything over 5 psi overpressure can cause burst eardrums and haemorrhaging.

P

P

PAL acronym for permissive action link. A remote digital code lock system on nuclear weapons that ensures that a bomb or warhead accidentally dropped does not detonate, although some release of radiation is generally seen to be inevitable. PAL equipment works with a code that is frequently changed and that may also destroy the weapon if unauthorised arming or detonation is attempted.

PAR acronym for Perimeter Acquisition Radar.
See **NORAD**

parity a situation whereby two hostile nations can offer equal military capability in the case of a struggle between them; this is especially applicable to the superpowers. Parity does not mean equality; it is judged by the size of retaliatory blow one nation can deal its opponent, and exists when neither side can see a major advantage to be gained in taking on the forces of the other. One of the main problems of such a theoretical position is that of actually counting and then verifying the respective arsenals. The counting of launchers, for instance, rather than the **MIRV**ed warheads they contain can create highly divergent sums. In addition, the nature of the two strategic triads is very different: the US has only 25 per cent of its **ICBM**s in silos, the Soviets have 75 per cent; the US puts far greater emphasis on strategic submarines; and so on. The nature of the arms race is such that neither side wishes to settle simply for parity but trades on national paranoia to work constantly towards gaining an edge. President Reagan's **SDI** can be seen as the extreme example of this continuing search for superiority. In the eyes of many experts, even actual equality, were it achieved, is not necessarily stabilising; it could be that such balancing of forces would in itself provide absolute justification for a nuclear trial of strength.

passengers the nuclear warheads carried by the rocket **bus**. When the bus of a **MIRV**ed missile arrives over the targets it manoeuvres from one to another, launching its various nuclear passengers as it goes.
See also **ICBM, MIRV, MARV**

PAVE PAWS acronym for Precision Acquisition of Vehicle Entry – Phased Array Warning System.
See **NORAD**

PBW acronym for particle beam weapons. High-energy, sub-atomic particle beams generated by huge nuclear accelerators of hitherto unprecedented power and designed for use as anti-ballistic missile weapons. Supporters of space warfare envisage such platforms dominating the earth from the high altitudes. Space PBWs are the stuff of true science fiction; as far as any development schedule might be considered, they are due to follow the laser weaponry (**SBL**) into the arms factories. Such PBW development as does exist is strictly ground-based. The initial research by one Nikola Tesla, a Bosnian, in the 1890s was laughed into ignominy by the US Patents Office. The concept vanished until 1977, when it was announced by the Pentagon that the USSR had developed a 'death ray', a PBW that could neutralise US **ICBM**s and alter the whole military situation. An article in *Aviation Week* revealed a 'fusion powered magnetohydrodynamic generator' based at Azgir in Kazakstan, powering the PBW. The CIA classified Azgir as URDF-3 (Unidentified Research and Development Facility 3). The USAF intelligence branch dismissed the whole incident as a possible underground nuclear test. Under investigation by the Joint Committee on Defense Production the story was generally dismissed. The rumours persisted, especially when the Swiss reported signs of airborne nuclides of unknown origin, that might have been blown from Azgir. On the whole, PBW for Russia or the US remains near the realms of fantasy, though if developed it would undoubtedly be deployed. All services are keen to have it; but it would appear that lasers dominate the current state of the military art. However, since laser developments are dominated by USAF research, the US Army has taken on such PBW programmes as exist. Development of a proton beam which would destroy incoming missiles was started in 1977, but such beams are susceptible to the earth's magnetic field which deflects and renders them inaccurate. Further researches, intended to overcome this drawback, are concentrated on the White Horse programme (formerly called Sipapu, after the Indian word for 'sacred fire' but then altered to protect ethnic sensibilities). This weapon will use a neutral particle beam, unaffected by the earth's magnetic pull.

PD-59 acronym for Presidential Directive No. 59. President Carter's executive order, signed in mid-1980, which supposedly redefined US strategic doctrine in terms of 'limited options counterforce targeting' and in calling for the first time on US forces to enable themselves to fight an enduring and protracted nuclear war. The Carter campaign of 1975 promised a reduction of US forces to **minimum deterrence** levels – some 200 missiles, carried on **strategic submarines**. He implied that the standing doctrines, summarised in Secretary of Defense Schlesinger's NSDM-242 of 1974 (derived in turn from his 'NU-OPTS' study at the RAND Corporation) would be dismantled. In the event the supposedly 'soft' President turned bellicose. Influenced by the hard-line Presidential Foreign Intelligence Advice Board (a Republican committee whose 'Team B' claimed, in the face of a far more pacific assessment of Russian aims by the CIA's National Intelligence Estimate, that the Soviets could and would make a **first strike**) Carter turned tough. In 1978 he set up a study to research three areas of possible action: a nuclear strategy that would eliminate the USSR as a functioning entity; the possible promotion of separatist movements within the USSR which might destroy areas that back the incumbent government; the identification of targets that would 'paralyze, disrupt and dismember' the Soviet government by annihilating the ruling group. PD-59, which summed up Carter's newly hawkish posture, certainly drew on the third of these. There were three major facets of the order: targeting was substantially changed from economic to military, leadership and command and political targets; Schlesinger's demand that any US strike should disable 70 per cent of Soviet industry was abandoned; for the first time there was posited the concept of a protracted nuclear exchange. Carter claimed no great novelty for PD-59. His Secretary of Defense Harold Brown stated 'PD-59 is not a new strategic doctrine; it is not a radical departure from US policy . . . It is in fact a refinement, a codification of previous statements of our strategic policy' and stressed that previous administrations had wanted to end the black-and-white simplicities of **MAD** and expand the nuclear options.

As far as the revision of targets went, Brown was right. **Counterforce** targeting had long been established; all that PD-59 had done was to create more 'packages' of targets and define more specifically the precise weapons configurations that would be used against them. This 'limiting' policy was linked to a belief that it would provide greater 'damage limitation', i.e. if no Soviet cities were targeted, then the Russians would not target any cities in the US. The proximity of both powers' civilians to most counterforce targets was ignored. Where PD-59 was new was in the demand for **survivability**, for the long-term nuclear war. Not a 'winnable' war; the Carter team never claimed that. But if the lengthy war was not presumed winnable, then it could only be seen as prolonging the nuclear agony. The US, come what may, was to create a 'victory-denying' response to any Soviet attempts to gain superiority in such a 'limited' war. Projections apart, the practical side of this survivability was to be obtained by the development of new weapons – especially **Trident** and **MX** – and a massive updating of **C^{3}I**.

PD-59 was aimed at two audiences, US and Soviet. Neither were impressed. The propaganda coup for which Carter hoped appealed neither to his conservative critics – who voted against him in 1980 – nor to liberals who deplored the new sabre-rattling. The Russians were equally dismissive; threats to use new weapons to eviscerate their command structure, destroy their troops and promote the counter-revolution held little force if those new weapons were unlikely to be deployed for at least a decade. The main beneficiary of PD-59 and the **countervailing strategy** it created was Ronald Reagan. For all his campaigning against Carter's weakness, Reagan's own policy (significantly absent in 1980) has been heavily dependent on the Carter plan. The main difference has been that, while Carter never openly promoted a 'winnable' nuclear war, the Reagan White House seems convinced of such a phenomenon.

See also **countervailing strategy**

Peacekeeper
See **MX**

penaid abbreviation for penetration aid. Any device, destructive or otherwise (such as metal **chaff** that distorts radar signals), that is used to guide missiles onto their target.

PEPE acronym for Parallel Element Processing Ensemble. A US army program for linking together the mass of computers required to process, analyse and respond to the information gained from the mass of US surveillance and sensor input. PEPE will coordinate between 300 and 900 minicomputers, all feeding into a massive mainframe machine. The new system will operate at 800 million instructions per second – more than adequate to deal with the estimated 12 million instructions per second that are required to track 200 targets, and the 30 million instructions per second proposed for ballistic missile defence.
See also **ABM, HIT, HOE**

personnel reaction time the time that elapses between the warning of a nuclear attack and the implementation of full defensive (and retaliatory strike) measures on an airbase, ship, command post, etc.

PGM abbreviation for precision guided munitions. Mass-produced, often lightweight or hand-held, armaments such as anti-tank or -aircraft missiles. With increased destructive power and flexibility of use (from air, sea or land), they have vastly increased the vulnerability of many formerly 'impregnable' targets. The Exocet missile of Falklands fame is a typical PGM. With an increasing use of radar and infra-red sensors, such weapons are revolutionising the contemporary battlefield.

PGRV acronym for Precision-Guided Re-entry Vehicle. Renamed Advanced Manoeuvrable Re-entry Vehicle (AMARV).
See also **ASMS**

piggy-backing the flying of a spy plane on an identical path to that of a legitimate civil flight so as to merge the radar profiles of the two aircraft and thus confuse ground-based spotters.

pin-down the concept of saturating enemy missile bases with so many warheads that the resulting electro-magnetic confusion will render their out-going guidance systems useless. While this theory may be technically feasible, it would seem that were so dense a barrage to fall, the bulk of the missiles would anyway be destroyed in their silos, making the status of their guidance systems largely irrelevant.
See also **EMP**

planning continuum Pentagonese for military strategy.

PMALS acronym for Prototype Miniature Air-Launched System. The state-of-the-art US **ASAT** system which the USAF has been testing for future use. This system comprises a two-stage rocket – made from two existing designs, the Boeing Short Range Attack Missile (**SRAM**) and the Vought Altair-3 – which carries the Miniature Homing Intercept Vehicle (**MHIV**) which actually destroys the target satellite. This composite missile is linked by a special pylon to its launch platform, the McDonnell Douglas F-15 fighter. The whole assembly can be attached to any F-15 by a kit which takes only six hours to install. The complete missile is just under 18 feet long and 20 inches in diameter; it weighs 2,600 lb. The first ASAT F-15 squadron was scheduled for deployment in 1985 at Langley and McChord Air Force Bases in Hampton, Virginia, and Tacoma, Washington. Targeting for PMALS is controlled by **SPADOC** at Cheyenne Mt, Colorado, where current surveillance systems are being updated to achieve maximum efficiency for the system. PMALS is a flexible system which gives the enemy a minimum of warning time in which to react. Its main drawback is part of this flexibility; to attain sufficient altitude to threaten many Soviet satellites, it requires a far weightier launch platform, which in turn would negate its manoeuvrability and relative invisibility from scanners that can spot an **ICBM** launch.
See also **ASAT, MHIV**

point defence the defence of a specific geographical point – in nuclear scenarios a complex of **ICBM** silos, a strategic bomber

airfield or a hardened command bunker. Given that such defence exists simply to ensure that the missiles, planes or bunker can survive a **first strike** and then retaliate, point defence has a strong element of **deterrence**. The US plans for an extensive development of ballistic missile defence (**BMD**) will concentrate on point defence.
See also **area defence**

point target a target so small and specific that it requires only a single coordinate on a map, e.g. a missile silo complex.

pop up
See **cold launch**

porcupine a proposed, but subsequently abandoned, defence system for the MX missile. Defences would send up a curtain of steel pellets or darts to deflect/detonate incoming Soviet missiles before they destroyed the US silos.

positive control the sending of nuclear bombers to a holding position, when alerted by warning of a possible missile attack, and the subsequent dispatch of those bombers onward to their targets, or recall of them to base if the warning proves unsubstantiated.
See also **fail-safe**

post-attack blackmail a tactic for waging nuclear war which is designed to minimise defensive damage while maximising **first strike** offensive damage. Ideally the first strike should concentrate on **counterforce** targets only, sparing civilians as far as possible; it should then be made clear that a further strike will destroy towns and cities unless surrender is immediate. Given the military realities this scenario, with its assumption of saintly docility on the part of the bombed country, seems highly optimistic, even during the era of **massive retaliation** when the US could claim nuclear superiority over the Soviets. In the event, both sides do possess the tools of nuclear blackmail, but only as **MAD**, a situation in which the threat, not the actuality, of attack can prove sufficient for **deterrence**.

post-launch survivability the ability of a given weapons system to deliver its bombs on target after having penetrated the enemy's defences.
See also **pre-launch survivability, survivability**

post-SIOP that period after a nuclear war has begun and the war plans have been put into operation.
See also **SIOP, trans-SIOP**

P

post-traumatic neurosis the current euphemism for the problems that engulf a soldier whose mind has, in the long or short run, been overwhelmed by the stresses of battle. It may be reasonably assumed that for all its technological artefacts, the effects of the nuclear, and possibly chemical/biological, battlefield will be if anything greater than those of any previous wars. This 'neurosis' is merely the most recent of many predecessors – shell shock (World War I) and battle fatigue (World War II, Korea).

posture a nation's current military strength and readiness as far as such factors affect its ability to fight a war.
See also **capability**

pre-emptive strike a surprise attack. To attack the enemy before he has a chance to appreciate that you have commenced the encounter.
See also **anticipatory reaction, anticipatory retaliation, splendid first strike**

preferential defence a defence plan that concentrates on certain key areas – military, government, industry – at the expense of those considered less 'valuable' – population centres with no important personnel, etc.
See also **point defence**

pre-launch survivability the ability of a given weapons system to ride out a pre-emptive **first strike** and then to retaliate successfully against enemy targets.
See also **post-launch survivability, survivability**

prevail to win a nuclear war. The concept of fighting and winning a nuclear war has developed gradually from the assumed US victories of **massive retaliation** through President Carter's **PD-59** to President Reagan's belief in limited wars and **graceful degradation**. Such a concept appears to defy all but the most blinkered analysts of what is most likely to happen once the powers begin swapping missile strikes; it stems, perhaps, from a mixture of the necessary bravado of all sabre-rattling foreign relations and the inescapable influence of the military-industrial complex, a force that exists as visibly in Russia as in the West. Like so many other aspects of the nuclear debate, the idea of prevailing can only be put to the ultimate test and as such continues to exist only by default. It is a concept, however, that is intrinsically more dangerous, and if it persists more likely to be put to the test, than the more esoteric suppositions as regard **fallout**, **nuclear winter** and the like.

See also **countervailing strategy**

preventive war the concept that war is inevitable and that, given this fact, one may as well get on with it as soon as possible and do one's best to win it, whatever the horrors and suffering involved. The prevention here is of defeat, not of conflict itself.

proliferation the mass-production and the possession of nuclear weapons by an increasing number of nations. Such nuclear capability does not have to come directly from the provision of actual weapons by the US or USSR; 'peaceful' nuclear reactors require plutonium and that same plutonium can be, and has been, diverted to warlike uses.

See also **Non-Proliferation Treaty**

proportionality the concept that, while European forces alone could not do as much damage to the Soviets as could the US, they could still inflict substantial damage and make the Soviets think twice about attacking Europe. As General de Gaulle put it, the European forces could 'tear off an arm'.

PVO Strany acronym for Protivovozdushnoi oborony strany, the Soviet National Air Defence Command. Commanded by an air force marshal, the PVO controls 550,000 men, 7,000 warning radars, its own air force of 2,500 aircraft (including eight different grades of interceptors and the Soviet equivalent to **AWACS**, the Moss), more than 10,000 surface-to-air (SAM) missiles and, in the **Galosh** deployment around Moscow, the only active anti-ballistic missile (**ABM**) system in Russia or the US. Whether the sixty-four-strong Galosh system could actually protect Moscow is debatable, but it does force the Western planners to target more **ICBMs** in that area than would otherwise be necessary. One drawback of the Galosh, which bedevils any ABM, is that their nuclear warheads, which are designed to destroy in-coming missiles through explosive power rather than spot-on accuracy, will not only destroy everything within a radius of several miles, but will create a cloud of electrically charged particles that will jam all adjacent radars. In theory the first Galosh might destroy its target, but in so doing it would 'blind' its own radar defences. The effect of a high-altitude explosion is also the creation of a massive and destructive electromagnetic pulse (**EMP**) which would destroy power supplies and thus much of the military communications structure. PVO Strany depends on its radar systems, backed up by early warning satellites, to provide the necessary early warning of any hostile attacks. At least one of the SAMs – the SA-5 Gammon – has anti-missile capabilities and, if activated by a warning from the PVO radars, could be used to shoot down high-flying missiles at a range of up to 100,000 feet. The whole SAM system has its faults – notably a lack of manoeuvrability, an inadequate guidance system and insufficient ability to deal with the mass of electronic counter-measures (**ECM**) used by US bombers.

Q

Q clearance the highest US government security clearance, which includes access to classified information regarding nuclear weapons.

R

race track (*or* multiple protective structure (*or* shelter)) one of the temporarily most popular, but ultimately rejected, plans for the unsolved basing of the mobile **MX** missile. Following plans for a 'vertical shelter' complex (also known as MAP – multiple aim point – which would require hostile saturation bombing to ensure the destruction of one missile) which was in effect a silo system, it was decided to create a cheaper and less technically demanding basing scheme. That vertical shelters could offer 50 per cent **survivability** (100 out of 200 MXs deployed on site) under a barrage of 20,000 Russian missiles was discounted. In their place came the race track or MPS basing. The 200 MXs were to be sited each on a 10–15-mile-long closed-loop road, equipped with twenty-three spurs leading in turn to shelters spaced approximately 7,000 feet apart and hardened to 600 psi. The number of loops per complex varied according to terrain, from three to seven, thus making a total of forty MX sites, all of which were to be built in Utah and Nevada. The missile would be carried around its loop by a transporter-erector-launcher, the TEL, a six-axle, twenty-four-wheel 670,000 lb vehicle, capable of carrying the 190,000 lb missile plus its 140,000 lb hardened **modesty shield**, masking the TEL from satellite sensors, but equipped with four 'plugs' which could be opened as and when required for **SALT** verification. Two modes of operation were envisaged: in one the missile moved periodically, spending most of its time in a given shelter; in the other the vehicle kept in constant motion around the track, 'dashing' at 15–20 mph into a shelter when an attack was due. In September 1979 President Carter renamed 'race track' 'sheltered road mobile system' and announced that the constant motion plus alert dash would be the optimum basing mode. By 1980 vociferous local opposition in Nevada and Utah made it clear that the tracks must be abandoned. Thus the project, estimated at a cost of $30–60bn over twenty years,

making it possibly the greatest construction project ever envisaged, was shelved. A number of variations on race track were suggested, none were taken up, and the problems of MX-basing, and indeed of the missile itself, moved on.
See also **CSB, MX**

RD acronym for restricted data. Any information about the design, manufacture or use of nuclear weapons. Such information is classified under the US Atomic Energy Act, 1946. In fact the material is never actively classified; the very fact that it falls in this area renders it automatically secret from the moment of its inception.

RDSS acronym for Rapidly Deployable Sensor System. A surveillance system, due to become operational by 1990, based on a series of buoys holding passive sensors that can be simply and speedily deployed by ships, aircraft or submarines in specific areas during times of crisis. The system was due to reach the last stages of development in 1977 but it was halted before this stage was reached, possibly to incorporate a new advance in sensor technology.
See also **ASW**

ready room an area, usually a hangar, where military hardware, especially missiles and other unmanned vehicles, are prepared for use, launching, etc. Particularly common on warships.

red box the safe, identically constructed on submarines, bombers and missile launch command posts, where the **go codes** are held in the event of nuclear war.

reliability the predicted percentage of missiles that will reach their target after they have been launched. The reliability of US missiles varies between 75–80 per cent; Soviet missiles vary between 65–75 per cent.

retaliation a nuclear attack launched by one nation as a reply to an earlier attack by another, i.e. a **second strike**. Whether or not they espouse the concept of 'limited' 'winnable' nuclear wars, most nuclear strategists are determined that if the other side starts the battle, then their forces must retain the capability of retaliation. For the West the usual picture is that the Soviets will launch a pre-emptive **first strike** – a surprise attack – and US and NATO forces will then respond in kind. That such a posture claims an essentially defensive role in no way curtails the offensive potential of Western arms. The need, given Western claims of 'fair play' against the duplicity of what Mr Reagan called 'the evil empire', to concentrate on retaliatory strength means that the arms, and their defences, must not only be capable of punishing the aggressor, but must first survive the attack. It is the retaliatory capability that underlines the endless stand-off that, for all its evolving nomenclature, maintains the uneasy balance between the superpowers.

See also **deterrence, survivability**

RISOP the Russian equivalent of **SIOP**.

rock any projectile: shell, rocket, missile, etc.

rope a type of anti-radar **chaff** that consists of long strings of metallic foil or wire which is designed to confuse the guidance systems of missiles and the radar scanners of planes, ships or land installations.

See also **penaid**

runway masher any weapon that is designed and targeted for the destruction of hostile air bases. Such a role is among those destined for the **cruise missile**.

S

SAC acronym for Strategic Air Command. SAC (motto, 'Peace Is Our Profession'; emblem, a mailed fist on a blue sky, three red lightning bolts and a green olive branch) was established in 1946 within the USAF as an elite nuclear strike force. With a fleet of B-36 and B-47 bombers, replaced from 1956 by B-52s, under General Curtis LeMay, SAC developed quickly from a somewhat ragbag group to a highly trained and motivated force which could, as LeMay put it, 'deliver an atom bomb to any spot on earth where it may be required'. As SAC commanding general, LeMay headed the Joint Strategic Target Planning Staff which selected the list of targets for US nuclear warheads as well as creating the war plans that evolved into the series of **SIOPs** that dictate overall US military planning. So powerful was LeMay from 1951 to 1955 that he was never required to reveal these plans to the Pentagon. Instead he announced target lists and the endlessly increasing bomb requirements to service them. By 1956 there were some 5,000–6,000 listed Soviet targets, of which SAC claimed bombers could hit 1,700. LeMay's 'optimum strike' employed a 700-warhead attack delivered by bombers over a two-hour period during which they were instructed to 'bomb as you go'. This very **massive retaliation** gave USN Captain William Moore 'the final impression . . . that Russia would be nothing but a smoking, radiating ruin at the end of two hours'. Ostensibly the US sought only **second-strike** capability, but LeMay (later celebrated in the Vietnam era by the ironic slogan 'Bombs Away With Curt LeMay!') was less squeamish. 'Our job,' he wrote in his memoirs, 'was to produce. And we produced. We put America in that situation of incipient power which she occupied at the time.' And which, it might be assumed, LeMay felt she ought to have used. While there was no actual proof, LeMay promised complete victory over Russia in thirty days, just half of what had been estimated when he took over SAC.

SAC today, operating from its hardened headquarters at Offutt Air Force Base near Omaha, Neb., has responsibility under commanding general Bennie Davis for two feet of the **strategic triad** – strategic bombers and missiles, which forces account for 50 per cent of the US nuclear arsenal. The bomber fleet comprises 165 B-52G and 190 B-52H bombers, all adapted to carry **ALCM**s and **SRAM**s as well as their traditional nuclear-armed gravity bombs. Up till 1968 the bombers maintained constant airborne alert but a number of near-disastrous crashes curtailed that programme. Since then the planes remain on ground alert, their crews on seven-day shifts, confined to barracks and sleeping near their aircraft. For all their updating, the B-52 is an ageing airplane. Manpower is short, the planes somewhat rickety and perhaps 25 per cent are under repair or crewless at any one time. Until the **B1-B** and **Stealth** (Advanced Technology Bomber) are deployed, the *status quo* will remain. Yet the bombers, anachronistic hangovers from a less technological age for many critics, fulfil a vital role; of all bomb delivery systems, they alone can be recalled. They also provide small and random targets, and can fly low enough to avoid radar until the last 4–5 minutes of their flight. On the other hand they are slow and ponderous, and vulnerable, once spotted, to anti-aircraft defences, as was proved over N. Vietnam.

SAC is similarly responsible for the US **ICBM** armoury, a mixed force of Minuteman III and Titan II missiles, manned and operated by some 71,000 personnel. Under a war alert SAC would operate from its underground bunker at Offutt, as well as from the **Looking Glass** plane, the flying command post that carries identical equipment and which, it is hoped, would survive the attack which, for all its hardened bunkers, is now presumed to destroy SAC's ground installations. SAC also controls the **ERCS** rockets, giving automatic pre-programmed launch orders from above the atmosphere. A computerised targeting system (SACDIN – SAC Digital Network) now ensures that, while missiles cannot be recalled, they can be re-targeted even when in flight, thus avoiding wasting bombs on empty silos or vacated airbases.

Ever since the LeMay era SAC has been a major influence on the collection of intelligence, both as to potential military targets (the current version of SIOP-5D lists some 40,000!) and

Soviet troop dispositions. Early development of US **elint** and **comint** was inspired by SAC, and since the late 1970s the USAF generals have consciously steered all strategic surveillance towards the preparation and implementation of the current version of the SIOP. SAC itself is responsible for strategic aerial reconnaissance, which is carried out by the SR-71 (Blackbird) and TR-1 (an updated version of the U-2s of the 1950s) high-flying spy planes as well as Air Force satellites. Under General Davis, who places **C³I** firmly at the top of SAC planning priorities, the Command's intelligence sources have expanded to include the hitherto sacrosanct **sigint** Special Intelligence, formerly the exclusive fief of the National Security Agency but now, like all other information, grist to the SIOP planning mill.

safing the reduction of (nuclear) weapons from a state of readiness to fire back to a safe condition once the emergency that caused their arming is considered to have passed safely.

SALT I acronym for Strategic Arms Limitation Talks. (Coined by Robert Martin, a junior member of the State Department Bureau of Political-Military Affairs when the talks were first being arranged in 1968. US diplomats deplored the acronym, but when the CIA adopted it officially within their filing system, it was accepted.) The talks lasted from 1969 to May 1972, when Richard Nixon and Leonid Brezhnev signed three major documents. (1) Basic Principles of Relations between the USA and USSR. (2) The Anti-Ballistic Missile Treaty. This prohibited deployment of **ABM** systems by either superpower, either on a full or partial territorial basis. ABMs were to be limited to two sites; the respective capital city and one **ICBM** complex in each country. Additional qualitative and quantitative restrictions were placed on ABM-related radars. (3) The Interim Agreement and Special Protocol on Strategic Offensive Missiles. This covered land and sea-based ICBMs and **SLBM**s. The aggregate total of strategic weapons was frozen for five years; a nation could mix its SLBMs and ICBMs as it chose, but the total limit could not be exceeded. A division was made between 'light' and 'heavy' weapons – the US had already begun to discard its ageing Titans, but the USSR still held on to some 308 huge SS-18s. Either party could give six months' notice and quit the agreement. Verification of numbers would be by 'national technical means' – spy satellites – and no deliberate concealment would be permitted. The protocol dealt strictly with strategic submarines, limiting the US to 710 launchers on forty-four **SSBN**s, the Soviets to 950 launchers on sixty-two SSBNs.

Even for its supporters SALT I was a disappointment. There were various mistakes, to be seized upon by left- and right-wing critics. In the first place it was interim, due for revision in five years. In putting limits on missiles it had ignored the whole concept of actually reducing the forces of assured destruction; in taking the launcher rather than the missile or the warhead as the unit of accounting, it had opted for ease of verification – missiles and warheads could be hidden, silos could not – but neglected the advance of technology, particularly **MIRV**ing (well-established in the US), which made a mockery of counting silos or SSBN tubes. There were no limits established on research and development, either of current or future weapons and both sides, while promising to abide by the five-year freeze, continued planning for new generations of technology. Finally, the ABM Treaty, the one supposed breakthrough, was little more than the mutual playing of a useful bargaining chip. Neither side wished to elaborate on these costly systems: both were satisfied to sacrifice them as a gesture to *détente*. By July 1974 the number of ABM sites was reduced to one only per country. Hard-line US critics condemned the Treaty as 'an historical mistake' which tied US hands indefinitely. Even as the treaty was signed, the chief US negotiator made it clear to the Soviets that, were there no further talks on arms limitation after five years, that would be sufficient reason to abandon the agreement. In the end SALT I existed as a prompt to further arms talks. Such talks were feasible; they could produce some form of agreement. The problem was to keep the ball rolling.

See also **SALT II, SALT III, START**

SALT II the second instalment of the Strategic Arms Limitation Talks (SALT II) commenced in March 1977 when Cyrus Vance and Vladimir Semyonov met in Geneva to start working out a successor to **SALT I**, which was due to expire in October of that year. Many critics on both sides felt that new talks would achieve little real change, but while *détente* remained popular it seemed necessary to keep some form of talks in progress. Initially the terms were to be a development of those agreed at Vladivostok in 1974. But the Carter Administration hoped for an improvement on that Accord, which in many opinions had merely given both sides *carte blanche* to continue with unrestricted arms development. In the five years of SALT I, arms technology had changed: missiles were more accurate; many of them were **MIRV**ed; even hardened silos were no longer proof against attack and both sides looked to mobile missiles to counter the new **CEP**s. It was vital to take this into consideration. Some experts remained optimistic; the Soviets had substantially narrowed the military gap since SALT I – they would be more willing to make concessions as near-equals to the US.

The broad basis to the talks was nuclear force parity. The intent was to equate the number of US MIRVs with the USSR's **throw-weight** superiority. Talks were further complicated by the balance of the respective **strategic triads**: US forces were divided 47 per cent **SSBN**s, 30 per cent bombers, 23 per cent **ICBM**s; the Soviets had 9 per cent SSBNs, 16 per cent bombers and 75 per cent ICBMs. Trade-offs would not be simple. The further complexities of **cruise missiles**, developments of specific warheads, the Russian **Backfire** bomber and the US F-111, and the various strategic forces of the NATO alliance were set aside, despite their importance to the overall strategic balance, to a proposed **SALT III**. The Russians rejected Vance's initial suggestion of all-round ICBM/SLBM cutbacks. As usual, each side's mathematics presented themselves in the inferior role. As the talks proceeded through 1978, it became apparent that there was as much opposition to Carter's initiative in Congress as there was to Vance's proposals in Moscow. An increasing distaste for *détente* and for Carter's Presidency made SALT II less and less popular in the US. The hard-liners, led by Florida's Senator Jackson, claimed that no treaty would be sufficiently verifiable, citing a number of alleged Russian breaches of SALT I. Carter's stance on linkage – demanding that the Soviets adhere to human rights positions and reduce their imperial ambitions in the Third World – merely irritated Brezhnev, as well as Carter's more sophisticated advisers.

But a treaty was worked out. In June 1979 the two leaders

met in Vienna to sign SALT II. It ran to one hundred pages, nineteen articles and one protocol. The major terms were as follows. By 1981 both sides were to accept a limit of 2,400 missile launchers each (to be reduced to 2,250 by 1985), of which a maximum 1,320 could be MIRVed. Of this total, only 1,200 could be ICBMs (maximum 820 MIRVed). Maximum MIRVS per missile were to be ten per ICBM, fourteen per **SLBM**. There would be no changes for the 308 'heavy' Soviet SS-18s. No bomber could carry more than twenty-eight **ALCMs**; **GLCMs** with range of 500+ km could be tested but not deployed until 1982. No new land-based missile sites could be built, but each side could develop one new ICBM and unlimited SLBMs. In a private letter Brezhnev promised to limit Backfire bomber production to thirty a year and to restrict them to medium-range activities. Both sides promised to work towards a Comprehensive Nuclear Test Agreement, a Non-Proliferation Treaty, an ASAT Treaty, a pact on Mutual and Balanced Force Reductions and the general restraint of world-wide sales of conventional arms.

SALT II found few friends in the US. While the joint chiefs accepted 'a modest but useful step' they saw no threat to their current arms programmes. The Pentagon's main fear was not of the Russians, but of the US civilians – cushioned by treaties, it was felt, the politicians and public might not even bother to develop to the full those weapons that were permitted. General Edward Rowney, a dissenting member of the negotiating team, saw the evident Russian advantage in throw-weight as 'a **window of vulnerability**' – a coinage that dominated arms planning for several years. The right resented agreements that left Russia strong, the left a treaty that made no difference to the arms race. But the real enemies of SALT II were the very factors that had promoted the talks. The expansion of Russian imperialism, unfettered by any threat of linkage, the hostage crisis in Iran, the actual invasion of Afghanistan and the potential one in Poland, plus the fear that the Soviets might finally achieve technological parity, united opponents in their vilification of *détente*. 'A temporary aberration' said the new President, Reagan, who called for military spending of more than five times that of the Vietnam War at its peak and declared 'any controversy now would be over which weapons the US should produce and not whether it should forsake weaponry for treaties and agreements'. The psychological scars of Vietnam and Watergate were to be forgotten; *détente* equalled weakness to an America that wanted to stand tall again. Finally there was President Carter himself. By 1980 he could claim little popular support; his image was of weakness, vacillation and ultimately failure. SALT I – Richard Nixon's treaty – was acceptable; SALT II – Carter's botched effort – was not.

See also **SALT I, START**

SALT III acronym for Strategic Arms Limitations Talks, part III. The round of arms talks that were scheduled to follow on from the **SALT II** talks that had ended with the unratified agreement of 1979. These talks were intended, *inter alia*, to consider the problem of intermediate-range weapons based in the European theatre. Although President Reagan announced in 1980 'As President, I will make immediate preparations for negotiations on a SALT III Treaty. My goal is to begin arms reductions', there were no immediate developments. In the event SALT III as such never materialised. Instead the abortive **INF** and **START** talks were commenced, neither of which managed to achieve any real progress.

S

salted weapon a nuclear weapon whose explosion will yield more than the average levels of radiation.

SAMOS acronym for Satellite and Missile Observation System. One of the three military satellite programmes developed in the wake of the Sputnik I launch in 1959, intended to initiate a satellite reconnaissance programme. Initially called 'Sentry', the SAMOS programme was launched in January 1961 when a satellite was put into earth orbit for twenty days, radioing detailed inventories of Soviet **ICBM** sites and general military topography. SAMOS was the first satellite to give detailed information on Russia from remote sensors, instead of relying on U-2 spy overflights, or even **humint** spies working from within the country. Such phenomena as the 'bomber gap' vanished once the facts were available. SAMOS satellites were too small to carry the increasingly powerful surveillance equipment; today they have been replaced by the three spacecraft of the Defense Support Programme.

See also **MIDAS**

sanctuary radar long-range air defence radar that does not reveal its presence to approaching aircraft and thus can neither be jammed nor attacked.

sanctuary strategy the concept of a European nation, most obviously the UK since it is an island, using its nuclear capability to persuade the Soviets to attack a lesser, weaker member of NATO. In essence this implies disloyalty to NATO and the opting out of a war to which one is bound by a treaty, but can be rationalised by the role that the UK has in acting as a staging post for US forces on their way to Europe. The importance of the UK to the US war effort is also seen as a reason for the Soviets holding back – attack the UK and the US will certainly take steps to defend its 'unsinkable aircraft carrier'. Conversely, the fact of being a US staging post must make the UK a prime target for Soviet missiles, aimed to disable its use as a forward base.

See also **second decision centre, trigger theory**

saturation attack an attack intended to overstretch enemy defences and to knock out as many as possible suspected or actual targets.

SBL acronym for space based lasers. The research into the possibility of laser-equipped space stations acting as ballistic missile defences (**BMD**) and anti-satellite weapons (**ASAT**). The first laser (light amplification by stimulated emission of radiation) was fired in 1960; by 1962 **DARPA** was researching its military applications. In 1975 a killer laser was tested against an airplane, in 1978 against an anti-tank missile; both experiments were reportedly successful. Since then DARPA has concentrated on developing chemical lasers which are ideally suited to space where their by-products need cause no harm, and the vacuum in space permits a concentrated beam of energy to travel very long distances without dispersal. Supporters of the militarisation of space, who include President Reagan since his **Star Wars** speech of March 1983, the USAF's **spacemen** and a number of conservatives in politics and the academic-military-industrial complex, hope to see a laser-based BMD system which will, they believe, put paid to **assured destruction** for ever.

DARPA is currently working on three programmes towards this development. Alpha is designed to produce a 5 megawatt (5 million watt) space-based laser which could damage satellites and high-flying aircraft. It has been estimated that the destruction of an aluminium-skinned missile in one second would require a 100 megawatt laser 'pump', and that laser would be required to destroy perhaps 1,000 missiles in the five to eight minutes that represent the vulnerable boost phase of Soviet missile launches during which an infra-red sensor system would be able to track and target the flaming rockets. On the basis that a laser converts 30 per cent of its fuel energy into beam energy, some 4,400 lb of fuel are required to destroy each missile. A fleet of even fifty of these 'battle stations' (and the realistic fleet might total 250) would require more than 1 million lb of fuel, a bulk that would need 2,750 shuttle trips to be placed in polar orbit. Obviously such a system would require a whole new means of space transportation. Counter-measures to ward off lasers are already being developed. They include an 'ablative' substance, which evaporates under the laser beam, revealing the shiny aluminium beneath, which in turn reflects the laser harmlessly away. Other schemes include the constant secretion of an ablative liquid, absorbing the laser energy and protecting the missile, or the constant spinning of the missile, thus exposing each part of its area for the least possible time. None of these methods is fully proven, but they are equally feasible and, like so many counter-measures to advanced technology, much cheaper to perfect than the system that necessitated them.

DARPA's LODE (Large Optics Demonstration Experiment) is developing a huge but lightweight mirror – 13.1 feet in diameter – of as near as possible optically perfect glass which will steer and control the laser beam. It will be manufactured in sections and assembled in space. Even this mirror will not be large enough for actual operations; the BMD battle stations will need mirrors some 49.2 feet (15 m) across and even the scheme's supporters have to admit that no nation as yet has the capability of manufacturing such a mirror.

The final programme, Talon Gold, is developing a low-power pointing and tracking laser which will locate the target and aim the laser. Its sensors, based on the same technology as used by NASA's space-based infra-red telescope, will be searching for targets between 600 and 3,000 miles away, requiring accuracy to 1/100,000 of a degree. Once spotted, the laser must slew round to fire on target. All this must be accomplished up to 1,000 times in a maximum of eight minutes. The Department of Defense has admitted that there are no plans as yet for an operational version of so sophisticated a tracker. Such a system would have to defeat the various simple but effective means of foiling it – the launch of fake missiles, phoney infra-red emissions from earth, even a small earth-based laser aimed to 'blind' it.

Further vital capabilities for an operational laser system would include a means of assessing actual kills, damaging hits and hits that merely pushed an **ICBM** off course. Some form of **C³I** would have to be established between the laser, the mirror and the tracker. The beam itself would have to be perfected against 'jitter' – the dispersal of its energy prior to reaching the target. If the full 'star wars' system was to be achieved, there might be some 2,500 battle stations, each of which would need to be inter-linked in one command and control system. The complexity of this would defy human abilities and even if a program could be written to work the system, it would exclude any human interaction with the battle stations. For the first time a weapons system would be autonomous, an experience beyond the conception of any military planners. Time and economic factors add extra burdens: developing one research system will take nine years; an operational system some twenty-five years. Costs are optimistically put at $500bn; with overruns and inflations, one trillion ($1,000bn) might seem more realistic.

The whole SBL program seems highly conditional, requiring breakthroughs in science and technology that rival any similar developments in the fields concerned. Yet one aspect remains concrete: the vulnerability of such a system. Any space-based weapons platform is an easy target. Even discounting the idea of rival space-lasers fighting their high-altitude battles (no doubt creating, with their deployment, a 'laser gap'), there are simpler methods – **fellow travelling** space mines, miniaturised high-speed interception vehicles (**MHIV**) and, simplest and most effective of all, a high-altitude nuclear explosion. Even before Mr Reagan's 'Star Wars' speech, the experts of the Pentagon, of DARPA and of the Defense Science Board all concurred, reluctantly or otherwise, in a rejection of a massive development of space-based lasers. The President's speech changed all this. The experts may still disagree, but the Administration, and those who will benefit – in status, in funds, or in glossy new weaponry – appear to be having their way. Star wars, once merely a Hollywood fantasy, seems on target for some form of actuality, thanks to the screen's arguably most successful actor.

See also **BMD, SDI, star wars**

SDI acronym for Strategic Defense Initiative. In a speech on 23 March 1983 President Reagan announced his plan for a radical alteration in US strategic planning; the creation of a massive ballistic missile defence system (**BMD**) designed to protect the US by shooting down hostile missiles before they could reach their targets. Promising a 'new hope for our children', Reagan called upon US scientists to help render nuclear weapons 'impotent and obsolete'. His Utopian visions were embellished in August 1983 when he promised to offer the SDI technology, once developed, to the Soviets; this allegedly would negate any ideas of US superiority and create a peaceful world of mutually assured security (**MAS**). Reagan consulted neither the Pentagon nor **DARPA** on his proposal, and although Administration ranks duly closed in support, even the closest advisers were initially surprised. Cynics suggested that SDI, with its enormous research budget of $30bn, was designed merely as a smoke-screen for an overall increase in defence spending, particularly on the much-maligned **MX ICBM**. After his speech, the President set two groups of experts to report on it, looking into defensive technology and future security strategies. Neither was impressed, but Administration spokesmen parroted their boss. A visiting Caspar Weinberger told Europeans of 'a thoroughly reliable defence' and Under-Secretary for Defense Fred Ikle promised 'The SDI is not an optional programme at the margin of the defence effort', dismissing critics who saw it as a new bargaining chip – 'It's central.' In essence SDI meant the end of the **ABM Treaty**, the single most effective limitation yet agreed on the arms race, and the replacement of the subtleties of diplomacy and arms talks, which had never appealed to Reagan, by one simple solution, practical or otherwise. Like the **zero option**, a similarly 'all or nothing' response to arms negotiations, SDI had initial public relations appeal, but fell apart under critical assessment.

Supporters of the project come from predictable areas. The military-industrial complex and the neo-conservative intellectuals liked both the appeal of a programme that seemed, if perfected, to return the US to the unrivalled superiority of the 1950s, and the massive budget, estimated in full at a possible one trillion dollars, in which there would doubtless be shares for all. A defence industry investment counsellor now runs a newsletter on SDI called *Money From Heaven*. The services, while split between the USAF, who regarded anything that flew as their province, and the USN, which is concentrating on the **Trident** programme and want an **ASAT** Treaty to protect its **NAVSTAR** guidance system, saw the formation of new command structures with their concomitant postings for the ambitious. Less enthusiastic were the European governments. In the first place **star wars**, as the media termed the futuristic weaponry proposed for the SDI, would not extend to their cities and populations. Fears of a **Fortress America** policy, of serious **decoupling**, were intensified. Following the remark of one administration official, who felt that while European support could not be bought 'it could be rented', a sop was offered in the form of defence contracts for European industry, although the work involved is strictly low-level, dealing only with unclassified items. Some European nations – notably Norway, Holland and Greece – have already rejected any participation in such researches, decrying the implicit militarism.

Serious critics of the SDI, such as defence expert George W. Ball, who has called the scheme 'one of the most irresponsible acts by any head of state in modern times', see two areas of difficulty – politico-strategic and technical. SDI will not, they say, create an era of international peace. Instead, with the repudiation of the **ABM** Treaty, an all-out arms race will be launched. Accuracy of weapons will no longer be necessary; missiles will be bigger and more plentiful, aimed strictly at defeating a BMD by sheer weight of numbers. On these terms, 'star wars' will give the Russians an immediate advantage – boosting the **MIRV**s on their 308 giant SS-18s to the potential thirty apiece will give them an important strategic edge. Since the Soviets are unlikely to wait for the US to give them their own BMD, their instinct must be to outwit it. In the final assessment, since, for all US protestations, the ultimate effect of such a foolproof defence must be to give the holders a real **first-strike** capability (they can fire their missiles, then use the BMD to destroy the retaliatory strike), the Russians may prefer to launch their own first strike, pre-empting any possibility of a US attack. If nations feel that they can dispense with **deterrence**, then such controls that do exist over potential conflict are drastically and dangerously weakened.

The technical flaws in the SDI are equally damaging to its success and usefulness. In the first place, the realisation of the BMD will require breakthroughs in eight key sciences, each one equal to or greater than the results of the Manhattan Project (the US wartime project that created the first atomic bombs) itself. This is problematic enough, but even with the breakthroughs, the system is imperfect. The Union of Concerned Scientists, in their *Report on Space-Based Missile Defenses* of April 1984 and their statement 'Why Star Wars Is Dangerous and Won't Work' (*New York Review of Books*, 14 February 1985), isolate the problems. (1) Underflying – neither **cruise missiles** nor strategic bombers, both of which systems fly much lower than the ICBMs at which star wars are aimed, can be harmed by the new BMD; on the other hand they can seriously damage the highly vulnerable satellites, laser 'battle stations', particle beam weapons (**PBW**) command posts, computers and other parts vital to the system. (2) Overwhelming and outfoxing – the easiest way to defeat BMD is to over-stretch its resources. By increasing the MIRVs per launcher and the penetration aids and decoys accompanying those warheads, the Soviets can put a 'threat cloud' of perhaps a million objects into space, each of which has to be analysed by BMD computers and, in the case of actual ICBMs, destroyed by a star wars weapon. (3) Technology – the computer hardware capable of performing billions of operations per second will soon exist, but can the software program be written to perform all the necessary tasks without error? Can the algorithms – the rules or criteria which govern the functioning of the computer-driven sensors at the heart of the BMD and which are built into the system at the outset – be guaranteed to work perfectly? And finally, how can a system of this immense complexity be debugged and tested outside an actual war, when there will be no time for alterations? As well as the computers, the proposed weaponry – the lasers and PBWs – remain nearer to science fiction than to military fact. Apart from their cost, anything based in space is highly vulnerable, these delicate assemblies more than usually so. (4) Institutional momentum – the massive SDI budget means that those who benefit from it are unlikely to let such funds go easily; irrespective of the real uses of star wars, and of its potential for destabilising the nuclear balance, the corporate and individual gains from so great a military contract will be exploited to the full, criticism notwithstanding.

To sum up the SDI, in the words of the Union of Concerned Scientists: 'Will we have reached the promised land where nuclear weapons are "impotent and obsolete"? Obviously not. We (will) . . . have a defense of stupefying complexity, under the total control of a computer program . . . whose performance will remain a deep mystery until the tragic moment when it would be called into action.'

See also **BMD, High Frontier**

SDS acronym for Satellite Data System. A USAF communications system specialising in polar communications. Four satellites in a Molniya orbit (a highly elliptical orbit, named for the Soviet satellites that pioneered it, which varies between a perigee of 200 miles from the earth and an apogee of 24,000 miles) move around the earth twice each day, spending half the time over the US, half over Russia.

second decision centres the concept that the use of nuclear weapons might be decided upon by a British government independently. This naturally assumes some limits on the traditional US–European consultative mechanisms and targeting plans. This implies two things: that the nuclear guarantee offered by US 'extended deterrence' is by no means trusted in the UK; and that there exists in British minds a situation in which the UK might wish to fight a nuclear war while the US refuses to. The overall aim is supposedly to complicate the calculations of an aggressor when deciding whether or not to launch a nuclear attack and to make it clear that, while the US might be reluctant to fire, the UK would not be. Such a scheme has the charm of allowing the UK an independent force, while being touted as benefiting NATO. The slightly sinister aspect of this policy is that this determination to control nuclear first use hardly fits in with the proclaimed UK policy of a purely defensive role for any UK deterrent. It does fit, as has been noted elsewhere, with the purchase of the **Trident** system, described by Robert Aldridge (1983) as 'the ultimate first strike weapon'.

second order threat some theoretical but unspecified military struggle, cited as far as twenty or more years into the future, which is used both by the state and military-industrial complex to justify the endless and enormous government spending on building an ever-larger military machine.

second strike a reactive, retaliatory strike by one nation in response to the **first strike** of its opponent. Current Western thinking, or at least the overt propaganda created for home consumption, projects the Soviets as crazed ideologues, ready at a moment's notice to launch a surprise attack on the US and its allies, while NATO is forced to maintain arms strength and war readiness in order to meet this attack with equal, but strictly defensive, aggression. If and when the West sends off its **ICBMs** and bombers, it will never be before the Russians have fired first. While such theories pander to the ideologues of the West, more sophisticated analysts back up the idea of a Soviet first strike not by citing a bloodthirsty Russian leadership, straining to unleash their robotic hordes, but by claiming that so brittle is the structure of their forces that the sooner they use them, the less likely the whole edifice is to crumble from incompetence and corruption. The undeniable Soviet advantages in conventional forces along the East–West front-lines in Europe also bolster fears of a surprise invasion. Whether this guarantees a nuclear first strike depends upon which side of the border one stands. There is every likelihood that such conventional superiority, with its gradual attrition of NATO defences without any need for theatre or strategic nuclear use, will be met by the firing by an increasingly desperate West of nuclear weapons. Such, anyway, is current NATO policy. And for all that Mr Reagan can hope for a limited, controlled nuclear exchange, few experts believe that once tactical weapons are used, global strategic ones can be far behind. Thus also 'second strike capability': the ability of the nation launching the retaliatory strike to use enough of its arsenal that has survived the first strike to make the retaliation hurt. This is further refined as 'second strike counterforce capability': the use of surviving missiles (current US thinking looks to the mobile **MX** and the highly accurate **Trident** II) to strike back at military targets. Such missiles are due to be launched in the period after the **NORAD** sensors have detected incoming missiles – the trans-attack period – and in some cases after those missiles have impacted – the post-attack period. From the Russian point of view it is these same Trident and MX missiles that assure them that it is the US that is pushing for first- rather than second-strike capability. Add to these super-accurate missiles the defensive umbrella of **star wars**, which aims for absolute US security, and the implementation of a US first strike appears, to those who wish to see it, as almost inevitable.

S

See also **first strike, pre-emptive strike, survivability**

security dilemma the driving force behind the arms race. Since one power fears the weapons of the other it adds to its own arsenal, believing that only by this attempt to gain the advantage, which the first power promotes as a purely defensive measure, can it maintain its own security. The second power can only see this increase in weapons as offensive, and thus reverses the situation, pulling ahead once more in the arms race, once again claiming that its new systems are purely defensive. The first power, seeing this, chooses to believe that its opponent is only building up for an attack and then reinforces its already modernised arsenal. This process can, and perceptibly does, dominate the relative arms programmes of the US and USSR, with one side gaining a momentary advantage, only for the other to develop suitable counter-measures and a new generation of weapons. The neatness of the equation is somewhat disturbed by the different national styles – the US concentration on submarines, the Soviets on silo-based missiles, the US liking for **MIRV**ing and miniaturisation, the Soviet belief in massive **throw-weight**, etc. – but the basic rules stand.

SEEK FROST
See **NORAD**

SEEK IGLOO
See **NORAD**

SEEK TALK updated air-to-air and ground-air communications systems for the USAF which will permit ground controllers and aircraft to communicate by UHF despite hostile jamming. This will be achieved by modifying existing UHF voice radios and adding up-to-date radar antennae.

seven-tenths rule based on the fact that many isotopes have very short lives, the estimation that by seven hours after a nuclear explosion the amount of radiation is only a tenth of the amount that it was immediately after the explosion.

severe damage the most extreme category of bombing effect assessment made by **SAC** pilots. The target has been reduced to dust. Lesser categories are moderate damage (reduction to gravel), light damage (reduction to rubble).

Sherwood forest the rows of Polaris missile tubes on a nuclear submarine; these tubes are painted green.

SI acronym for special intelligence. Information collected by **sigint** but kept apart from other varieties of military intelligence. The staff of SI installations, controlled by the National Security Agency, are more heavily vetted prior to employment and are allotted higher security clearance than are other electronics intelligence personnel. SI personnel number 25,000 in Washington DC and a further 100,000 worldwide. SI secrecy extends to the department's funding, which is hidden inside the larger Defense Department budget. SI costs (1983 figures) $13bn per year, with a further $10bn spent on reconnaissance, early warning, base maintenance and salaries. This top-secret intelligence gathering is controlled and processed by the JCS Strategic Reconnaissance Center in the Pentagon, the National Military Intelligence Centre of the Defense Intelligence Agency (DIA), the CIA HQ at Langley, Va., and the National Sigint Operations Center of the NSA at Fort Meade, Maryland. Although SI was formerly the private property of the NSA, the continuing attempts by **SAC** to influence all intelligence agencies has meant that recently a combination of SAC planners, in tandem with **C³I** experts, have forced the NSA to let them use this vital material.

See also **sigint**

SICBM acronym for small intercontinental ballistic missile. Given the continuing inability of the Pentagon to opt for a basing system for the **MX**, as well as Congressional reluctance to vote money endlessly for its development, and the realisation that the once invulnerable **ICBM** silos are no longer able to withstand increasingly accurate hostile targeting, the US is seeking a new and more flexible missile system. A variety of missiles are under consideration – the **Midgetman**, the Pershing III and the eponymous SICBM. Such 'mini-missiles' would be spread over the Western US, some in silos, some with a mobile transporter-erector-launcher (*see* **race track**). Each missile would carry a single warhead of between 300–500 KT. These missiles are envisaged as a back-up rather than a replacement for MX, and deployment of approximately 3,000 is scheduled for the 1990s.

See also **Midgetman**

sigint abbreviation for signals intelligence. The electronic monitoring of Soviet signals traffic for the gathering of information regarding military and political developments. Sigint is under the control of the National Security Agency (NSA), established in 1952, which coordinates the sigint of all three US services. Sigint maintains a network of eavesdropping posts around the world, tuning in to Soviet transmissions. Anything in the fields of codes, cryptography and communications security also falls to sigint monitors. The NSA, with, and independently of, the CIA, also deals in phonetaps and general communications interception abroad, usually using diplomatic cover. There are some twenty-five NSA-controlled sigint stations around the world, including sites in Germany, Great Britain, Italy, Turkey, Diego Garcia, S. Korea, Puerto Rico and Panama.

See also **comint, elint, humint, SI, telint**

significant quantity that amount of uranium-235 required to make an atomic bomb.

SIOP acronym for Single Integrated Operational Plan. The all-embracing military contingency plan that covers the deployment and use of the US nuclear forces, as well as those of the UK. So secret is this plan that it has been given its own security classification – ESI, Extremely Sensitive Information. The first SIOP, completed in 1960, was a development of the **SAC** targeting plans assembled by a succession of SAC commanders in the 1950s. It was revised under President Kennedy as SIOP-62 and again for President Nixon in 1972. The current plan, SIOP-5D, was issued in 1980, the direct result of President Carter's **PD-59** which, among other policies, first stated clearly the policy continued and expanded by the Reagan Administration – the concept of the 'endurable' and thus 'winnable' nuclear war. SIOP-5D has escalated the 4,000 targets of 1962 (even then a vast case of overkill, since it has been estimated that the destruction of a mere 232 targets will cripple the USSR) to an absurd and inflated 40,000 targets. Given that the US can at maximum strength and efficiency only muster 10,000 warheads capable of reaching the USSR, and that there is no guarantee that all of these would impact as predicted (indeed, unless the US forces were 'fully generated' (on a war footing) already, only about 50 per cent of the missiles would even be ready for launching), such a list seems utterly implausible. Nonetheless SIOP planners have created a range of **attack options** for the Commander-in-Chief, with major, selected, limited and regional targets, plus two special categories which deal with both pre-emptive and retaliatory (**launch on warning**) strikes. Built into the fine-tuning of the strike options are various options such as 'withheld' targets – command bunkers, **C³I** nodes, urban centres, etc. – which, were the plan to perform as desired, might be spared in an initial strike, with the intention of using their possible destruction as a threat to force the Soviets to surrender. Ignoring the niceties, the 40,000 targets are divided into four main sections. (1) Soviet Nuclear Forces – 20,000+, including conventional targets; **ICBM**s, **IRBM**s and their respective launch facilities and launch command centres; storage sites; airfields supporting nuclear-capable aircraft; **SSBN** bases. (2) Conventional Military Forces – bases, supply depots, marshalling points, non-nuclear airfields, ammunition storage facilities, tank and vehicle storage yards. (3) Military and Political Leaders – 2000: command posts and key C³I facilities. (4) Economic and Industrial Targets – 15,000: war material and ammunition factories; petroleum refineries, railway yards, repair facilities. Urban centres are excluded from this **counterforce** targeting but, given the propensity of the Soviets to place ICBM silos near cities, this exclusion would be restricted to paper theories. As well as Soviet targets, SIOP has provision for theatre and strategic weapons in Warsaw Pact countries, Cuba, Vietnam and China, as well as some unspecified 'allied and neutral territory'.

See also **countervailing strategy**

sit position to collect strategic information in one of the many US bases devoted to electronic surveillance.

S

SLBM acronym for submarine-launched ballistic missile. SLBMs, the weapons that arm the sea-borne leg of the **strategic triad**, the strategic submarines, are those most likely to initiate a nuclear **first strike**, either on a limited theatre level (there are 400 Poseidon warheads aimed at theatre targets) or on a global scale. The flexibility and virtual invulnerability of a submarine ensures that not only can it elude hostile surveillance but it can station itself far nearer its targets than can a static silo-based **ICBM**. Thus while an ICBM takes some 30 minutes from launch to impact, SLBMs can cut this to 10–15 minutes, and using a low-line 'depressed trajectory' can avoid radar scanners for all but a few minutes of that, offering an enemy virtually zero reaction time. When **MIRV**ed and **MARV**ed these missiles have been rightly cited as 'the ultimate first strike weapon'. Despite this power, neither the US nor the Soviets are deploying SLBMs with true hard-target kill capability. The proposed Trident II missile is intended by the Pentagon to remedy this, but other SLBMs remain devoted to soft targets – cities, air bases, industrial complexes, etc. While the Russians have a larger fleet of SSBNs, they continue to lag behind the US in technology. Their inability to perfect a solid-fuelled SLBM continues to limit the vital **CEP** of the missiles. The chief SLBMs deployed or in development by the superpowers are as follows.

American. (1) Poseidon C-3. The 304 Poseidon SLBMs remain the chief USN strategic weapon. Deployed from 1969, to replace the ageing Polaris A-3, the Poseidons arm a fleet of nineteen Poseidon submarines. Each missile can carry up to fourteen × 50 KT MIRVs, but the usual figure, based on the unratified but generally accepted **SALT II** agreements, is ten. With a CEP of 450 m Poseidon is relatively inaccurate, but still quite capable of destroying soft targets. A single Poseidon submarine firing all its MIRVs can destroy 224 cities or moderately hard targets. (2) Trident I C-4. Development of a successor to Poseidon began in 1967, under the **Strat-X** program, when it was hoped to create a longer-range missile using existing or simply developed technologies to be deployed on the current submarine fleet. This ULMS (under-water long-range missile system) was put in abeyance during development of the new Trident submarine but once that program was well underway, EXPO (Extended Poseidon, as it was now called by USN) was reactivated. Testing for Trident I proved difficult and experts are still not fully satisfied with the need to link maximum use of microtechnology and lightweight construction materials with attaining accuracy and stability in flight. A number of experimental Tridents exploded in tests. Despite this, Trident I is now deployed. Twelve Poseidon submarines carry the missile, as do the first three Trident submarines. The Trident missile carries eight 100 KT MIRVs with a range of up to 6,900 miles. The CEP of 450 m still restricts targeting to soft or medium-hard targets. (3) Trident II D-5. The second generation of Trident missiles, due for deployment by 1988, represent the first SLBMs with real hard-target penetration. With a CEP of 133 m, the nine or ten 475–600 KT MIRVs (depending on the 'mix' chosen for a given vessel) can threaten silos and command centres anywhere in Russia. As President Carter put it, Trident II has 'significant hard target kill potential against time-urgent targets'. The intention is to build twenty-eight Tridents by the year 2000, with a potential of 672 launch tubes between them. For strategic planners the Trident fleet will give accuracy, flexibility, **survivability** and above all concentrated power: a fleet of nineteen Trident-armed submarines can attack 4,213 targets; the fleets of ten Polaris and thirty-one Poseidon submarines could between them only attack 3,907. It is also intended to add the Mk V Evader MARV to the D-5, giving it a CEP of only 20 feet.

Russian. After the debacle of the Cuban Missile Crisis in 1962, the Russians pledged themselves never again to permit

US missile superiority. To this end SLBMs as well as ICBMs were put into intense development. The Soviet Navy now deploys a large number of SLBMs of varying ranges and destructive yield. All of them suffer from two basic defects: the large CEP, which makes for inaccuracy and which the US shares; and the dependence on liquid fuels, which the US has surmounted. The main Soviet missiles are these. (1) SS-N-6 (Sawfly). The main Soviet SLBM: 384 are currently deployed on the fleet of Yankee-class submarines, sixteen missiles per vessel. Despite their importance, the missile has only a 1,300–1,600 mile range, and firing to hit **CONUS** targets would bring the submarines dangerously close to US waters, a policy usually deplored by Russian strategists who prefer longer ranges to avoid the mass of sophisticated American **ASW** technology. Like other SLBMs, the SS-N-6 has a poor CEP (900–1,400 m), threatening only soft targets with its 1 MT or three 350 KT warheads. (2) SS-N-8. The second most popular Soviet SLBM: 267 are deployed on the Navy's Delta-class submarines. Two versions of the missile can deliver either a 1 MT or 800 KT warhead. Range is 4,300 miles and CEP 1,300 or 900 m, depending on the version. (3) SS-N-18. Two hundred and eight of these missiles are deployed on Delta-3 submarines. Three versions exist: three 200 KT MIRVs with a CEP of 1,400 m over a range of 6,500 km; one 450 KT, CEP 600 m, range 8,000 km; seven 200 KT MIRVs, CEP 600 m, range 6,500 km. Essentially an upgraded SS-N-8, this missile remains liquid-fuelled, but offers a more sophisticated guidance system. (4) SS-NX-17. Only twelve of these still experimental missiles have been deployed. Their intent was to perfect a solid-fuel system, but after its initial appearance in the late 1970s production seems to have halted and the missile must be judged a failure. (5) SS-NX-20. Designed for the monster Typhoon submarines (one launched 1980, another undergoing sea trials in 1985), this as-yet-to-be-launched missile system will be solid-fuelled and, with an 8,000 km range, should be capable of hitting any target in the US. As a rival to the Trident I and II, the SS-NX-20 is expected to offer a payload and CEP accuracy far greater than other Soviet missiles. Full deployment is scheduled for the end of the 1980s.

See also **ICBM**

SLCM acronym for sea launched cruise missile.
See also **ALCM, cruise missile, GLCM**

SLC-6 (*or* Slick-Six) acronym for Space Launch Complex Six, sited at Vandenburg Air Force Base, Calif. Originally built by the USAF for launching its (now aborted) Manned Orbiting Laboratory, now under development as a launch pad for the space shuttle (the National Space Transportation System).

SMA acronym for standard metropolitan area. A figure used for the calculation of the numbers of deaths in a given level of nuclear attack; the USA, for instance, has fifty-three SMAs.

smart any form of precision guided munitions (**PGM**), especially those with built-in computers, variable radar frequencies, anti-jamming devices and similar means of avoiding electronic and conventional counter-measures and perfecting the weapon's ability to home in accurately on target, despite all the defences put in its way.
See also **dumb rock**

S

smart bomb any form of missile that uses built-in computers, variable radar frequencies, anti-jamming devices and similar means of homing in accurately on a target and eluding all the defences, electronic and conventional, that may be encountered.

soft any target that has not been specially hardened against the effect of nuclear blast. Human beings are the ultimate soft target, but any unprotected target – cities, air bases, factories, etc. – will succumb to the explosion.

SOSUS acronym for Sound Surveillance System. The backbone of the USN open-ocean sensing system – passive underwater listening devices (hydrophones) which are permanently fixed on the continental shelves of the US and its allies. The information elicited from these devices is sent to shore stations by cables. These cables are occasionally obstructed by Soviet 'trawlers', which search for them in an attempt to disable the communications. A fleet of US cable repair ships (T-ARC) counters such efforts. SOSUS was installed in 1960 and undergoes continuous improvements. When conditions are favourable it can spot a submarine anywhere in the ocean and pinpoint it to a 60 mile radius. It can also interact with **ASW** aircraft and escort surveillance ships. It is, however, sensitive to conditions and SOSUS is backed up by two further systems, **SURTASS** and **RDSS**.

See also **ASW**

spacemen members of the US military who advocate and develop concepts of 'space power' – the fighting of wars with space-based weapons and satellites. Spacemen believe above all in the great military potential of space, even to the extent that it will be from developments in space that there will spring ultimate power over events on earth.

See also **star wars**

S

SPADATS acronym for Space Detection and Tracking Stations.

See **NORAD**

SPADOC acronym for Space Defense Operations Center.

See **NORAD**

spasm war term coined by Herman Kahn in a series of briefings on war planning, delivered in the late 1950s. The final all-encompassing rung on the nuclear **escalation ladder** in which both sides abandon themselves to uncontrolled reflex attacks; goals, aims, plans and any similar modifications are all rendered irrelevant by this burst of emotional violence. 'Spasm war now has acquired the technical significance of an attack in which there is maximum effort in the first strike and little or no concern over later strikes. The objective is to achieve as much destruction as possible in the first strike without compromising other considerations' (H. Kahn, *On Escalation*, 1965).

spike the programming of two warheads to explode as nearly as possible at the same moment over the same target. This simultaneous explosion will multiply the destructive effects by far more than merely one plus one.

See also **cross-targeting**

splendid first strike a nuclear attack that destroys or cripples the enemy's potential for retaliation. Such an attack (as seen in the conventional sphere in the Israeli Air Force's devastating sorties against the Egyptian air bases that initiated the Six Day War in 1967) would appear only to work fully if coming with little or no prior warning. Given the general acceptance that the move towards nuclear war would be gradual (*see* **escalation ladder**), such a sudden blow might be unlikely. On the other hand, were one participant in the crisis to 'jump' several rungs of the escalation ladder, the requisite shock could be obtained. It is worth noting the use of the word 'splendid', an openly emotive word that would not usually be expected in the vocabulary of nuclear jargon and euphemism; obviously the delight of the planners in the success of an attack which, militarily at least, represents the absolute optimum of such plans, cannot be contained.

See also **pre-emptive strike**

SRAM acronym for short range attack missile. Air-to-ground missiles designed to destroy hostile ground defences, carried by B-52 and F-111 strategic bombers in addition to their warheads. Some 1,150 SRAMs are deployed on US aircraft, each capable of delivering a 200 KT warhead over a range of 50–140 miles, travelling at 2,000 mph and employing inertial guidance and terrain clearance sensing systems.

SRBM acronym for short-range ballistic missiles. A variety of land-based ballistic missiles, none of which have a range in excess of 900 km. The US and NATO deploy the Pershing 1A, Lance and Honest John missiles; the Soviets have SS-12, SS-21, SS-22, SS-23, Frog 7 and SS-1. Such weapons are reasonably mobile and, if the range is shortened, can double for medium-range missiles in dealing with most of the same targets. The SS-12 and SS-22 can hit 85 per cent of the targets in NATO assigned to the SS-20 once it has been moved forward into a Warsaw Pact country for launching. The US Pershing II, which can similarly substitute for Tomahawk (cruise), is viewed with equal misgivings by the USSR.

S-S acronym for surface-to-surface. The overall designation of Soviet ground- or sea-launched missiles. These are further modified by the addition of -N- for naval weapons and -X- for experimental missiles: thus the SS-18 (the Soviet 'super-heavy' **ICBM**), the SS-N-8 (one of the major Soviet **SLBMs**), the SS-X-24 (an experimental ICBM, possibly the equivalent of the US **MX**), the SS-NX-20 (the Soviet equivalent to the **Trident** I missile, scheduled for use on Typhoon class submarines), and so on. For details as to specific Soviet missiles, see entries under ICBMs, SLBMs.

See also **ICBM, SLBM**

SSBN acronym for ship, submersible, ballistic, nuclear. A nuclear-powered ballistic-missile submarine. For details of the respective fleets held by the superpowers, see **strategic submarines**.

See also **SLBM**

star wars the media nickname for President Reagan's Strategic Defense Initiative, launched in March 1983 and which promised the development of space-based missile defences, especially laser weapons aimed both at earth targets and at rival defences in space orbit.

See also **SBL, SDI**

START acronym for Strategic Arms Reduction Talks. On assuming office in 1981 Ronald Reagan declared 'My goal is to begin arms reductions', but practice lagged far behind this promise. If the new Administration possessed a foreign policy, it was to discredit and discard *détente* and all that went with it, notably the arms control of **SALT**. For their first year of power, the Reagan White House managed no more than a new acronym, START – and that, it would transpire, had been coined by Carter's adviser Zbigniew Brzezinski in 1977. But for Reagan's men, novelty was all: SALT was tainted, a new name was vital. 'Limitation' became 'reduction', a ploy designed to appeal to all views; liberals would welcome cut backs and the right, convinced that SALT had permitted the Russians to maintain superiority, would acclaim a treaty that decreased Soviet forces. A superpower meeting was set up for May 1982 in Geneva; what was needed was a policy to be used at it. Instead the US line was divided between the State Department, who essentially proposed a development of SALT, limiting missile launchers rather than sizes, and the

Pentagon, who wished to cut back **throw-weight**, the actual sum of Soviet explosive power. Both parties wished to deal with **MIRV** technology by setting ceilings for individual warheads too. Both plans, for all their different emphases, demanded much the same of the Soviets; they were to reduce their primary armaments – silo-based **ICBM**s which made up 75 per cent of their strategic forces – by as much as two-thirds, while US cuts to obtain a similar ceiling would be merely cosmetic. Such demands fitted in perfectly with current US plans for modernising their forces; they effectively froze Russian intentions. The National Security Council (NSC) devised terms of reference for START; equality (with the implication of pulling back a Soviet military advantage), stability (the end of the current US inferiority in the arms race), reduction (rather than limitation), deference to the concerns of the allies (i.e. compatibility with the INF talks), verifiability and sustainability. When an alliance of the Joint Chiefs and the State Department plumped for the launcher-plus-warhead rather than throw-weight option Reagan announced the US START position in a speech at Eureka College on 9 May 1982. Both sides would be restricted to 5,000 ballistic missiles, of which only 2,500 could be ICBMs; only 850 launchers would be permitted. A secret clause aimed to limit Soviet throw-weight to 2.5 m kg. Soviet 'heavy' missiles – SS-18s – were to be reduced from 308 to 110, and medium missiles – SS-19s – to 100. Even for proponents of the plan, it was hard to envisage any appeal in this for Russia. A week after Eureka, Brezhnev outlined the Russian stance for START: a freeze on all strategic arms, both in arsenals and under development. As biased in Russian favour – it would outlaw all US modernisation programmes while leaving Russia's throw-weight superiority untouched – as was the US proposal in America's, it did not suggest an easy round of talks. Brezhnev also intimated that if the US attacked the 'heavies' then Russia could challenge the US forward bases in Europe, which had been left out of SALT.

START lasted until November 1983, when the Russians walked out. The reasons for its failure were many. Mutual intransigence, compounded by a desire to put propaganda before policy by both sides, undermined attempts to create a useful dialogue. Polemics and sloganeering counted for more than the practical suggestions. The Russians loathed the hard-line US chief negotiator, Edward Rowney, veteran saboteur of SALT II, whom they categorised as 'a stubborn, stupid man, and a rabid opponent of arms control'. Rowney preferred to see himself as a tough old pro, a connoisseur of Russian duplicity and the hard-nosed front-man for a hard-nosed President. This was an illusion. Reagan certainly cast himself as a tough guy, but he continued to show himself embarrassingly lacking in understanding of even the simplest detail. He appeared to believe that US **strategic submarines** and bombers carried only conventional weapons; he worried that submarines might be 'sunk'; in 1983, under Congressional attack, he admitted that in his Eureka speech he had never appreciated its massive pro-American bias.

As the talks lingered through 1982, a desire emerged in the US to accelerate progress. The Scowcroft Committee, set up to investigate this, advised a softening of the US line; the 2,500 ICBM limit was scrapped, the 850 launcher limit was raised to 1,200, Russian 'heavies' could number 150. In Congress there emerged the concept of mutual **build-down**, whereby the introduction of every new weapon must be accompanied by the retirement of several old ones. Reagan himself liked this – it seemed to mix the Administration's desire for US modernisation with an apparent gesture towards reduction – but the Pentagon did not. The Russians merely commented 'Your idea of "flexibility" is to give the condemned man the choice between the rope and the axe.' In March 1983, bored perhaps by the START deadlock, Reagan announced his Strategic Defense Initiative, featuring space laser weaponry and dubbed by the press **star wars**. In mid-1983 James Goodby of the State Department was charged with making one last attempt to get START moving. His plan for substantial de-MIRVing, coupled with a new ceiling of 8,000 single-warhead missiles, impressed no-one. The in-fighting in Washington continued. A series of new proposals seemed only to insult the Russians further; 'Old poison in new bottles' said chief Soviet negotiator Viktor Karpov. In November 1983 Karpov and his delegation quit the talks. The supposedly revolutionary US approach to diplomacy and arms negotiations had failed. A mix of unrealistic demands, US in-fighting, Presidential fantasies, and above all the unchanging national aspirations and strategic doctrines of the superpowers had wrecked these talks as surely as they continue to do all others.

See also **SALT I, SALT II**

Stealth (*or* Advanced Technology Bomber – ATB) the development of 'Stealth' technology, designed to enable military ships, submarines and airplanes to avoid hostile radar scanners, was initiated by the Germans in World War II in an attempt to disguise U-boat periscopes. Since 1977 Lockheed, builders of the U-2 and SR-71 'Blackbird' spy planes, have been air-testing the ATB, a new bomber designed to augment the B1-B in replacing the ageing USAF B-52 fleet. The new aircraft will be lighter than conventional bombers and has a redesigned tail, high-mounted engines, heat-suppression devices and a carefully shaped airframe in which radar-reflecting 'corners' are eliminated as far as possible, thus deflecting radar beams to the side rather than sending them straight back to their source. The ATB has been built of non-metallic materials which render it 'transparent' to radar beams, which will pass through rather than bounce back from the airframe. The development of 'Stealth' remained classified until a leak revealed the new bomber in 1980. It is proposed that 100–150 ATBs will be deployed during the 1990s. Although the ATB is designed to take over from the B1-B, critics argue that the new bomber is unnecessary. The $40bn development budget is over-blown and the B1-B, which employs a good deal of the ATB's anti-radar technology itself, should be sufficient without a further aircraft. As of 1985, programmes have been initiated to enable both the ATB and the B1-B to acquire and engage relocatable targets, notably Soviet SS-20 and SS-X-245 mobile missiles.

See also **B1-B**

stockpile energy the sum of the total energy available for use in a major nuclear conflict. The international nuclear arsenal can be calculated at 20,000 warheads, yielding some 20,000,000,000 tons of TNT, the equivalent of 1,333,333 Hiroshimas.

strategic architecture the overall construct of nuclear war strategies, involving command, control and intelligence (**C^{3}I**), troop dispositions, targeting of hostile centres, etc.

strategic arsenals it is impossible to make an absolutely accurate assessment of the nuclear arsenals held by the two superpowers in their respective **strategic triads**, but the figures as of 1 May 1984 are included below. Given that both powers accept that for minimum **deterrence** a force of no more than 500 warheads is required, and that an effective **first strike** should require no more than 2,200–4,500 warheads, the near 19,000 warheads possessed by the two nations (not to mention the 35,000 tactical nuclear weapons for short- and intermediate-range use) present a case of massive **overkill**. The divisions of the weaponry as to launch platform and the relative concentration of numbers in the US and payload or **throw-weight** in the USSR further confounds the issue and helps the opposing negotiators create completely different answers to what might appear reasonably simple problems of addition.

See Table opposite.

All these figures are subject to variations and estimations, and are the admitted figures issued by the superpowers. They are, nonetheless, the most accurate summary of the strategic arsenal at the date compiled. *Source*: Paul Rogers, *Guide to Nuclear Weapons 1984–85*, The School of Peace Studies, University of Bradford, 1984.

strategic balance the comparative nuclear strengths of the two superpowers and their allies and satellites.

See also **balance of terror**

strategic bombing

See **SAC**

strategic connectivity the improvement of the command and control of nuclear forces to ensure that in the event of a nuclear conflict, despite whatever its magnitude and potential chaos, the **war-fighting** plans would proceed as scheduled. In the words of General Richard Ellis, Director Joint Strategic Connectivity Staff: ‘Once execution [of the Emergency Action Message (**EAM**)] is complete, we must have sufficient feedback and data intelligence information to evaluate not only the efforts of our retaliatory attack on the enemy but also our own resources remaining to continue the war . . . Finally, we need communications in the trans- and post-attack period to reconsti-

Delivery mode	Delivery system	No. of systems	No. of warheads	Sub-totals
US				
ICBM	Titan II	36		36
	Minuteman II	550	550	
	Minuteman III (1)	250	750	
	Minuteman III (2)	300	900	2,236
SLBM	Poseidon C3	304	3,040	
	Trident C4	288	2,304	
				5,344
Bombers	Gravity bombs and SRAMs	2,378	2,378	
	ALCMs	768	768	
				3,146
US total warheads				10,726
Soviet Union				
ICBM	SS-11	500	500	
	SS-13	60	60	
	SS-17 (1+3)	120	480	
	SS-17 (2)	30	30	
	SS-18 (1+3)	58	58	
	SS-18 (4)	250	2,500	
	SS-19 (1+3)	300	1,800	
	SS-19 (2)	60	60	
				5,488
SLBM	SS-N-5	9	9	
	SS-N-6	384	384	
	SS-N-8	280	280	
	SS-NX-17	12	12	
	SS-N-18	224	1,344	
	SS-NX-20	40	280	
				2,309
Bombers	Gravity bombs and ASMs	290	290	
				290
Soviet Union total warheads				8,087

tute our surviving forces, generate follow-on sorties and retarget our forces, as required. This complicated cycle is then repeated until hostilities are terminated.'

strategic nuclear weapons ostensibly those weapons, usually **ICBM**s, which can reach the enemy's home territory when fired either from the home territory of his opponent or, in the case of **SLBM**s, from a strategic submarine. Recently the increased accuracy of all weapons, and the development of intermediate range weapons, plus the deployment of intermediate- and short-range weapons along the East–West border and in NATO and Warsaw Pact countries, has meant that the line between strictly strategic and tactical weapons has been blurred. Given the continual refinements of missile technology, it may be assumed that this process will continue.

See also **tactical nuclear weapons, theatre armaments**

strategic submarines as opposed to the hunter-killer submarines which, like the surface warships operating above them, pursue and attack hostile submarines, the strategic submarine exists simply as a weapons platform, a superlatively mobile missile launcher, roaming the oceans at will, generally undetected for all the increasingly sophisticated anti-submarine warfare (**ASW**) techniques ranged against it. The **SSBN**, the naval 'foot' of both superpowers' **strategic triad**, is that most likely to be employed in the launching of a putative nuclear war, either on a strategic or a theatre front. The elusiveness of such submarines will also ensure that so long as communications can be maintained between them and such command posts as remain after a war has begun, they will be uniquely placed to continue fighting that war, even if land-based missiles have already rendered much of the earth a sterile desert. SSBNs are only limited by two drawbacks, both of which are in the process of being remedied: the above communications, which are still restricted by the nature of the sea itself; and the accuracy and **throw-weight** of the missiles deployed on them. In the communications area, the US at least hopes to render the oceans 'transparent' before long, with the development of **ELF** transmissions. In missile technology both powers are starting to deploy weapons – the US Trident II D5 and the USSR SS-NX-20 – which will have hard-target kill potential equivalent to that of the silo-based **ICBMs**. Even without such missiles, SSBNs can already destroy a wide range of soft to medium targets – cities, industrial centres, government centres, etc. – a Poseidon submarine, for instance, can target and destroy 224 cities. The current and proposed state of the respective strategic submarine fleets is as follows.

USA. (1) Poseidon. Deployed since 1969, the Poseidon replaced the now obsolete Polaris (only the UK still maintains a Polaris fleet, and its original Polaris A-3 missiles have been updated by the **Chevaline** programme). Based on King's Bay, Georgia, Charleston, S. Carolina, Holy Loch, Scotland, and Pearl Harbor, Hawaii, the fleet comprises nineteen submarines armed with sixteen Poseidon C-3 missiles and twelve submarines armed with sixteen Trident C-4 missiles. With an estimated 'life' of twenty-five years, the submarines will be phased out to be replaced by the Trident by the late 1990s. (2) Trident. Named for the water-god Poseidon's three-pronged spear, the Trident submarine represents the USN's desire to combine the proven flexibility of undersea operations with the accuracy of silo-based missiles. Developed from the **Strat-X** study of 1966–7, this weapons platform for the new Trident I and, in due course, Trident II, missiles went into prototype production in 1973. Troubled by development problems, such as the less than desired 'quietness' of the moving vessel and the instability of new steel alloys used in its construction, as well as those occurring in its complementary missiles, the Trident programme is well behind schedule. The first Ohio-class Trident went on patrol in late 1982; the 1985 fleet stood at three vessels, each armed with twenty-four Trident I C4 missiles (each carrying eight to fourteen MIRVs). It is intended that the full fleet of twelve Tridents will be afloat by late 1990; the ninth to twelth ships will come fitted with the Trident II D5 missile, the first **SLBM** capable of hard-target destruction, at which point the first eight will be backfitted with the D5. Trident is based in Bangor, Washington, supposedly thus forcing the USSR to maintain a watch on the Pacific as well as the Atlantic (although a Poseidon fleet is already based in the Pacific); the US is also negotiating for a new base in Micronesia (possibly on the Palauan Is.) and developing facilities on Diego Garcia in the Indian Ocean, leased from the UK and exclusively US military territory. Irrespective of base or missile, a Trident commander, it has been pointed out, is, after the US President and the Soviet Premier, the most powerful man on earth; his submarine contains more destructive power than the combined military arsenals of the UK, Italy, Spain, Brazil, Argentina, West Germany, Japan, the Philippines, India and Pakistan.

USSR. Piqued by their defeat in the Cuban Missile Crisis of 1962, the Soviets determined never again to fall behind the US in strategic missile strength. The crash programme that was then initiated included strategic submarines, but, while such weapons are perhaps the most vital in the US strategic triad, the geographical nature of the USSR – relatively landlocked, subject to frozen ports during winter and with its navy forced to pass through easily surveyed bottlenecks on the way to open water – means that SSBNs are accorded less importance in Soviet planning. A variety of submarines – Yankee-1 and -2, Golf-3 and -4, Hotel-3, Delta-1 and -2 – carry a variety of configurations of the main USSR strike missiles, the SS-N-6, SS-N-8 and SS-N-18. Like their US equivalents, such missiles are restricted to soft to medium targets; however their efficiency is further impaired by the inability of their designers to substitute solid for liquid fuel in their engines. In 1980 the USSR launched its answer to Trident, the gigantic Typhoon-class submarine, a launch pad for the SS-NX-20, a missile, like Trident I and II, designed to destroy important hard targets. The 33,000 ton displacement Typhoon dwarfs the 18,700 ton Trident, and can deliver SLBMs onto US targets without leaving USSR waters. Its warhead arsenal, nonetheless, remains at 240, far less than the Trident's potential of 336 (408 with Trident II). The SS-NX-20, like the Tridents, is by no means trouble-free, its main problem so far being to explode in flight.

See also **SLBM**

strategic superiority 'the ability to control a process of deliberate escalation in pursuit of acceptable terms for war termination. The United States would have a politically relevant measure of strategic superiority if it could escalate out of a gathering military disaster in Europe, reasonably confident that the Soviet Union would be unable or unwilling to match or overmatch the American escalation. It follows that the United States has a fundamental foreign policy requirement that its strategic nuclear forces provide credible limited first strike options' Colin S. Gray, Director of National Security Studies at the Hudson Institute, 1978.

strategic triad the tripartite military alliance which determines the military planning and strategy of both superpowers. Influenced by geography, national obsessions, technological developments, the demands of the respective military-industrial complexes and inter-service rivalries, the two triads differ in their composition. The US triad, in order of precedence, comprises: the Navy's missiles, **SLBMs** carried on **strategic submarines**; the USAF's missiles, carried by **ICBMs** based in their silos; and the USAF fleet of strategic bombers. The US Army, which has never really maintained its presence in the triad, is attempting to stake its claim with the Pershing II missile, supposedly capable of hitting Moscow if launched from W. Germany. The Soviet triad is dominated by the Strategic Rocket Forces, whose 1,398 silo-based missiles total some 75 per cent of the total USSR strategic strength (US ICBMs represent only 25 per cent of the national forces). Although the newest department of the USSR military, founded only in 1959, the SRF are known as the 'primary service' and its commander, who commands 413,000 troops, takes precedence over all his peers. Strategic bombers and submarines, neither of which have been developed to the equivalent US capabilities, divide the remaining quarter.

strategic warning a prior warning of imminent nuclear warfare that can be appreciated and supposedly acted upon weeks or even months before the crisis becomes insupportable and one side launches a **first strike**.

See also **escalation, tactical warning**

Strat-X the study of the potential direction of US nuclear arms planning instituted by the Pentagon in 1966 and carried out between 1966–7 by the Institute of Defense Analysis. The overall brief was to discover the ideal successors to the then current strategic arsenal, either through creating new technology or developing that which existed. The decisions taken through Strat-X led variously to the **MX** missile and the **Trident**

missile system with its submarine launcher as the twin spearheads of developing weapons technology.

surface burst a ground-level or extremely low-level nuclear explosion. In both cases the fire-ball touches the ground and produces a large crater and massive radioactive **fallout**.
See also **air burst, ground burst**

surge the ability of the USN to put all its strategic submarines to sea at once. The supposed response to a crisis.

surgical strike originally coined in Vietnam to describe an attack made for a specific, one-off purpose, destroying or concentrating on a specific target. The Israeli strike on Iraq's nuclear plant – which was felt to be making nuclear weapons rather than merely power – typifies such a strike.

SURTASS acronym for Surveillance Towed Array Sensor System. This surveillance system was made operational in 1980 and uses arrayed sonar sensors that are towed slowly through the oceans by tuna clipper-type boats. Data is broadcast from the towing ship to a satellite and thence to a shore station for analysis and processing. The complete SURTASS fleet will comprise eighteen arrays, complete with towing ships, codenamed T-AGOS and AGOS (air-to-ground ocean surveillance).
See also **ASW**

survivability
See **post-launch survivability, pre-launch survivability, survivable weapons**

survivable weapons weapons systems that can absorb a first or retaliatory strike and continue to operate as and when the military command wish them to do. The development of such systems accept the impossibility of a static target, i.e. a missile silo, withstanding the accuracy and **throw-weight** of current **ICBM** technology, and looks towards mobile missiles – the **MX** or SS-20 – and the arming of **strategic submarines** with **SLBMs** such as the Trident II D5 and SS-NX-20 which can combine their proven elusiveness with a still unachieved ability to destroy hardened targets. Survivable weapons are a vital concomitant of the current strategic doctrine of the 'winnable' nuclear war.

See also **post-launch survivability, pre-launch survivability, strategic connectivity**

swarmjet a defence concept for protecting US missile bases, especially those of the **MX** missile. Thousands of small rockets would be launched along the corridor through which it could be calculated that attacking Soviet missiles must fly; the rockets ought to destroy at least some of the incoming weapons. In the event swarmjet was abandoned, like many other plans, for MX, though to what extent this was because its deployment might well break the 1972 ABM Treaty was not stated.

See also **BMD, MX**

systems bargaining the preservation, during an **escalation** towards nuclear war, of precedents that reduce the likelihood of further escalation, and which place thresholds in the way of an eruption into war. 'A general expression for situations in which all or almost all members of a system would be better off if every individual abided by certain rules' (Herman Kahn, *On Escalation*, 1965).

systems engineering the organisation of building and installing a complicated piece of new military hardware.

T

TACAMO acronym for take charge and move out. A worldwide network of high-powered communications stations and a fleet of fourteen (to be increased to eighteen) specially equipped Lockheed C-130 transports which fly in relays twenty-four hours a day and which are used to pass on messages to the US fleet of strategic submarines by reeling out a 5.5-mile-long antenna for VLF communications. The planes are also equipped with satellite UHF communications. One aircraft patrols the Pacific, the other the Atlantic. The flexibility of these moving aircraft ensures that the equally flexible submarines remain on the move and stay extremely hard to track down. Some experts claim that any message to a submarine makes it potentially vulnerable to hostile sensors, but in the 2,000-plus patrols since the system was instituted in 1960 the USSR has failed, according to US Intelligence, to track down a single vessel. Current updating of the entire US **C³I** organisation includes plans to replace the C-130s with a more modern aircraft.

See also **MEECN**

tactical nuclear weapons short-range (up to 200 km) weapons also known as battlefield nuclear weapons. These include the US Army's Lance MGM-52C, the Lance II and Nike-Hercules MIM-14 artillery missiles, plus a number of artillery-fired atomic projectiles (AFAP), and two nuclear mines, the medium and small atomic demolition munitions (MADM, SADM). The USAF holds one air-to-air nuclear armed missile – the Genie AIR-2A. The USN has a number of ship-to-ship and ship-to-air missiles: specifically the Terrier RIM-20, the Standard 2 RIM-67B. The ASROC RUR-5A and SUBROC UUM-44A are anti-submarine warheads, both being scheduled for replacement by the **ASW/SOW**, a version of the Tomahawk **cruise missile**, which will have greater range and superior accuracy.

The Soviet Army deploys the FROG-7 (free rocket over ground), the Scud (SS-1B/SS-1C) and Saleboard (SS-12), which range from 40 to nearly 500 miles. All three are scheduled for replacement by 1990, respectively by the SS-21, SS-23 and SS-22 missiles. The USSR generally avoids nuclear capable artillery, with the single exception of the S-23 180 mm towed gun, although some pieces are reportedly under development. The Soviet Navy carries a large range of **SLCMs** in a ship-to-ship role, although they can be adapted for ship-to-ground use. The most important are the SS-N-3 (Shaddock), SS-N-7, SS-N-9 (Siren), SS-N-12 (Sandbox), SS-N-14 (Silex, the equivalent to the US ASROC) and SS-N-15 (equivalent to SUBROC), SS-N-19, SS-NX-21 (the equivalent to the USN's Tomahawk SLCM and as such virtually an intermediate range weapon) and the SS-N-22 (a development of the SS-N-9). The Soviet Navy also has the FRAS-1, anti-submarine rocket, nuclear torpedos and mines. The UK, whose forces form part of the NATO front line in the Central Sector, have the Lance missile, the M109 6-inch howitzer, the M110 8-inch howitzer and a number of US originated nuclear mines. Britain, Germany and Italy have combined to produce the FH70 and SP70 nuclear capable 155 mm howitzers.

See also **SICBM, strategic nuclear weapons**

tactical warning an alert immediately prior to a nuclear war which is given anywhere from days to minutes before that war breaks out.

See also **strategic warning**

target response the effect on troops, *materiel* and civilians of the blast, heat, flash and fallout from a nuclear explosion.

target servicing

(1) the attacking of a target with either nuclear or conventional weapons.

(2) the provision by military planners of worthwhile targets which have troops or weapons in place, or which present an opportunity to attack economic, communications or leadership centres or civilian areas, with the effect on morale that such attacks will have.

TEAL AMBER a proposed satellite-based surveillance system which uses a TV camera to 'stare' at an area of space and register the passage of anything that moves across it and immediately spot orbital characteristics, comparing these with previous sightings. TEAL AMBER will be so sensitive that it will be able, weather conditions permitting, to spot an object no larger than a dinner-plate up to 40,000 miles distant.
See also **TEAL RUBY**

TEAL RUBY
See **NORAD**

teeth arms those arms of the military services who actually engage the enemy – armour, infantry, battleships, etc.

teeth-to-tail ratio the ratio of actual combat troops engaged in fighting to those auxiliaries whom they require to sustain their fighting effort. The nearer one is to one's home territory, the smaller this ratio needs to be; thus German troops fighting in the Central European Sector (the East–West German border) will need far less 'tail' than do US troops fighting there, since the latter are 5,000 miles from home.

TEL acronym for transporter-erector-launcher.
See also **MX, race track**

telint acronym for telemetry intelligence. The tracking of and listening in to USSR missile tests.
See also **comint, elint, humint, sigint**

TERCOM acronym for terrain contour matching. A sensor system that acts as the 'eyes' of a **cruise missile** and backs up the in-built inertial guidance system. TERCOM follows a computerised map of the route to the target with virtually 100 per cent accuracy. The sensor also watches the ground below, giving cruise the ability to 'hug' the contours it overflies. In flight TERCOM continually compares its map, which is programmed into each missile according to its target, and the path the flight is actually taking; any discrepancies are automatically corrected and instructions executed by the missile's automatic pilot. The maps themselves, which include an estimated

100 million references at a cost of approximately $1bn for the entire cruise programme, are created by the Defense Mapping Agency, using satellite-borne devices. The collection of this mass of data has been in progress since 1975 and has made it possible to include **ALCMs** in the **SIOP**.

See also **cruise missile**

termination capability the ability of a nation or nations to bring a war to an end.

theatre the zone of combat and communications involved in a war, extending to the larger area that may be directly affected by the fighting.

theatre armaments (*or* theatre nuclear weapons) any nuclear weapons with a range of less than 5,500 km. These are further divided into: tactical weapons, with a range of less than 200 km and designed for battlefield use by troops, involved in a head-on conflict; intermediate-range weapons, with ranges up to 1,000 km; long-range or 'Euro-strategic' weapons, with ranges between 1,000 and 5,500 km. All these missiles are restricted only to range; they can, although the tactical weapons will not, possess warheads as large as those carried by **ICBMs**. The last category of missiles have confused the old division of nuclear weapons. Obviously NATO missiles sited in forward bases along the Iron Curtain need only medium to Euro-strategic range to penetrate into Russia itself; the Soviets cannot threaten US targets in the same way, although an attack with theatre weapons from Kamchatka could certainly penetrate Alaska. The various capabilities of nuclear-armed aircraft merely intensify the problems: an intermediate weapon carried by a long-range bomber can hardly be equivalent to its land-sited version; an aircraft based on a carrier cannot be pinned down to a specific base, and so on. Given the ever-increasing accuracy and proliferation of every degree of nuclear weapon, the real effect of this blurring of categories is to make harder and harder the search for meaningful arms control. For instance, to the Soviets these forward bases are another example of imbalance in US's favour; to the US it is vital to protect European allies from the ever-present Soviet menace.

The niceties of negotiation are made infinitely more complex when geography, as well as technology, splits the protagonists.
See also **strategic nuclear weapons**

threat assessment conference a check, of a maximum of three minutes duration, in which US **NORAD** commanders assess intelligence of incoming missile attacks and determine the suitable response. At current levels of **ICBM** technology, this conference leaves nineteen minutes before impact.

threat azimuth a missile launch that appears to have been fired on a threatening, warlike path, as opposed to test flights which can be determined as non-hostile.
See also **threat fan**

threat fan a multiple missile launch that has been computed by **NORAD** surveillance as being targeted on the US or its allies.
See also **threat azimuth**

T

three-D problem the assessing of missile targets by considering (1) detection, (2) discrimination, (3) destruction.

throw-weight the total weight of what can be carried by a missile over a particular range. The weight of that 'business end' (Talbott, 1985) of a rocket, including armaments and the guidance system that will deliver them on target once the launch vehicle has boosted the missile to the apogee of a ballistic trajectory and all other stages of the missile have been discarded. In older missiles the throw-weight was merely the warhead itself; modern **MIRV**ed missiles create a throw-weight that includes all the warheads, the post-boost vehicle (the **bus**), plus all necessary guidance systems, plus various electronic counter-measures such as metallic **chaff** and any other propulsion or penetration aids; unlike single-warhead missiles, most of this throw-weight neither lands on nor explodes on the target. In arms talks, it is throw-weight that is computed by the US to prove that the Soviets have nuclear superiority, epitomised by their 308 heavy missile launchers (the SS-18s). While **ICBM**s remained relatively inaccurate, the massive Soviet warheads did confer extra power (if one neglected that fact that both sides held huge enough arsenals to destroy each other several times, accuracy notwithstanding) and the US sought to control it. Throw-weight dominated the 1982 phase of the **START** talks, with US negotiators desperate to set a standard which would limit Soviet power. However, as technology advanced, so did the throw-weight imbalance matter less. Increased accuracy meant that a smaller weapon could yield destruction out of proportion to its throw-weight. If what matters is the destruction of **time-urgent** (hard) **targets**, then the US fears are spurious. Despite this, those who fear Soviet **breakout** (the ability to gain superiority while not transcending the limits of an arms agreement) still seek to limit Russian throw-weight. The Soviets, understandably, remain reluctant to accept throw-weight as a useful definition of relative strength and certainly show no signs of allowing the US to persuade them to limit this resource.

time-urgent targets (*or* time-sensitive targets) the highest priority targets. Any target that must be destroyed before it can elude an incoming missile: aircraft still on the ground; missiles still in their silos; command-and-control centres; munitions storage areas. Most of such targets are hardened and thus can only be attacked by **ICBMs** and not slower, albeit accurate, **cruise missiles** or strategic bombers. The new Trident II D5 missile is intended to create the first US **SLBM** capable of such 'hard target penetration'.

trans-SIOP a period during which the **SIOP** is being executed, i.e. a nuclear war.

Trident
See **SLBM, strategic submarines**

trigger theory the concept that, if such a situation were feasible, the early use of nuclear weapons by a small power would act as a trigger or catalyst for the subsequent developments of superpower relations in the crisis, i.e. once even small nuclear weapons had been used, how could the superpowers keep from unleashing a full-scale war? In the end this seems something of a deliberate 'scare' tactic, as no one is likely to appeal to any US government that is anyway less than confident in its

European allies and their 'worthiness' to receive US military hardware.

trip-wire force those ground forces which are stationed along what, in the case of war, would become a military front-line and which, from their immediate proximity to the first stage of a war, are generally seen as expendable. Their task would be to provide as lengthy as possible a period for other, more distant, forces to prepare for battle. The most obvious examples of such forces are the NATO troops in Germany; vastly outnumbered by Warsaw Pact forces, they could only provide short-term opposition in the case of a concerted attack. It is known that NATO war plans assume that once these troops have been eliminated, the use of **tactical nuclear weapons** is the next step. Given that the invading troops will be nearing the launch sites of such weapons, the policy of **use them or lose them** will take over, and the Soviet advance will be destroyed by bomber and missile attacks and shells from nuclear howitzers. It is likewise understood that the Soviets would not launch a limited retaliatory attack but move to a full strategic launch of **ICBMs**. The US would undoubtedly respond in kind.

two-man rule the rule operated by the US Strategic Air Command (**SAC**) to ensure as far as possible that one individual cannot trigger off nuclear war 'by mistake' or through an excess of drink, drugs, nervous tension or misplaced patriotism. This rule extends through all phases of nuclear weapons handling, from guarding them in storage to arming and actually firing them. A launch crew consists of two men – originally senior officers, USAF colonels in their forties, now junior officers, usually captains, in their mid-to-late twenties. As well as keeping a visual, and if necessary physical, check on their partner, the two men must combine in the turning of two keys simultaneously to operate the actual triggering mechanism that launches a missile. The stresses of such a job are so great that, despite special screenings and aptitude tests, the Air Force's entire complement of launch officers turns over every three years. In the Soviet Strategic Rocket Forces the desire to eliminate 'accidental' war is as hotly pursued. A Soviet launch crew comprises four men – two regular servicemen who launch the rocket, and two KGB soldiers who alone are permitted to arm it. In earlier years this procedure extended to keeping the warhead physically distant from the rocket, guarded by KGB men.

See also **ICBM**

T

U

unacceptable damage the concept that the damage one's own nation would suffer from a possible retaliatory/**second strike** would outweigh any advantage gained from launching one's own **first strike**. Quite what amounts to unacceptable damage is highly debatable. One scenario of the early 1960s, when US nuclear superiority was still unchallenged, envisaged a first strike on Russia which would engender, through retaliation, up to 15 million US deaths; this figure was considered by RAND corporation experts, whose calculations continue to have a major influence on US nuclear planning, quite acceptable. Today's planners of 'limited' nuclear war are similarly content to juggle with **megadeath** statistics that, if not desirable, are at least 'not unacceptable'. Given that the UK's Home Defence exercise of 1980 ('Square Leg') envisaged 29 million corpses plus 6.4 immediate casualties after what is generally assumed to be a likely attack on Britain of about 200 bombs, and that the UK's status as America's 'un-sinkable aircraft carrier' remains unchanged, the bounds of 'acceptability' must be drawn very wide.

See also **assured destruction**

use them or lose them the concept in nuclear **war-fighting** whereby a commander should fire his missiles, even in an uncertain situation, rather than wait and risk having them destroyed uselessly in their silos.

See also **attack options**

V

validation codes codes that authenticate each of a series of nuclear launch commands and assure launch officers, isolated in the control rooms of their silo complexes, that there is actually a war in progress and that finally they are to trigger and launch their missiles.

Vela the general designation for any nuclear explosion detection programme, whether space- or ground-based. Also used adjectivally to describe the 'host' satellites upon which the hardware responsible for executing such programmes is based.
See also **IONDS, MIDAS, NUDETS**

verification the checking by one partner in a treaty that the other partner is keeping to the terms of that treaty. As far as nuclear arms control is considered, verification is carried out by the spy satellites of each superpower. Verification is vital to the continued success of deterrence; a statement by the Arms Control and Disarmament Agency (**ACDA**) in 1980 noted 'The deterrent value of verification depends to a considerable extent upon the potential violator being ignorant of the exact capability of the intelligence techniques used to monitor his compliance with an agreement', but did add that 'verification contributes to mutual trust among the parties'.

vertical proliferation the upward spread of the numbers of nuclear weapons in the hands of the international fraternity of nations with nuclear capability.

VHSIC acronym for very high speed integrated circuits. Circuits that are extremely small and have the ability to process data extremely fast. All the services devote large funds to university programmes designed to develop VHSIC. Current research has produced chips a mere 2 and 1.5 microns wide (substantially thinner than a human hair). The goal of the Department of Defense is to reduce this still further to 0.5 microns. Such miniaturised, ultra-high speed processors are vital to the development of space-based reconnaissance and warning systems.

See also **ET, VLSI**

Vladivostok Accord master-minded by Henry Kissinger and signed by Gerald Ford and Leonid Brezhnev in 1974, the Accord was designed to carry **SALT II** negotiations through the hiatus caused by Watergate and President Nixon's resignation. Based on launcher totals rather than **throw-weight** as the unit of accounting, it established one aggregate for strategic ballistic missiles and strategic bombers (2,400), another for **MIR**Ved ballistic missiles (1,320) and a number of general principles, notably that the USSR could keep their 308 heavy SS-18s and that the US forward-based systems (**FBS**) would not be counted into assessing mutual strengths. Vladivostok saw the start of the **cruise missile** debate: the US believed that the Accord covered only high-trajectory ballistic missiles, while the Russians afterwards alleged that they had believed that air-breathing, low altitude missiles, guided from launch to target, were also included. The debate remains unresolved. Critics of the Accord claimed that it did nothing, merely permitted both powers to continue doing what their own research and development programmes were geared to do. There were no real restrictions on new generations or types of missile. As Vice-President Walter Mondale put it in 1977: 'It looked like both sides took their weapons programmes, stapled them together and called the result a breakthrough.'

VLSI acronym for very large scale integration. Integrated circuit fabrication technology that allows more than 100,000 transistors to be placed on a single chip. It is at the heart of the new weapons and surveillance systems developed for emergent technology (**ET**).

See also **VHSIC**

voting system a security system designed to prevent 'accidental' nuclear war. Bomber and missile silo launch crews must obtain coded correlation of launch plans from an outside source, without which they are unable to remove the locks on the nuclear bombs and missiles that they control. This system does not extend to the captains of strategic submarines, who have full power, in the absence of any corroboratory orders, to launch the missiles on their ship.

See also **ICBM, two-man rule**

W

war of resolution a term coined by Herman Kahn to denote a contest in which all restraints are abandoned in a 'naked matching of resolve with resolve in an exchange of exemplary attacks and reprisals' or, as he adds, 'a drive towards a show-down' in which presumably there will be a result, a victor and a loser.

war-fighting according to Herman Kahn (*On Escalation*, 1965) 'the term "war-fighting" is . . . an antonym of "spasm" or "deterrence only" in describing how a strategic nuclear war might start, be waged, and be terminated, and how post-war survival and recuperation problems can be handled.' In other words, war-fighting equates nuclear with conventional war, creating a system of tactics and plans that discount the overwhelming evidence that no-one can win a war in which nuclear weapons are employed and the general repugnance towards such a concept, outside government and the military, which such evidence produces. The paradox of nuclear arms – if no-one can win what is the use of their endless development and deployment? – is, of course, anathema to governments and to the military (and to their allies, the arms producers). Only by considering nuclear war as a somewhat more dramatic conventional one can the whole edifice be maintained. Thus war-fighting – the predominant policy of the Reagan administration and the justification for a wide-ranging arms and arms-related programme which includes the development of new arms, the updating of ageing forces, the massive revamping of **C³I** systems and, most recently, President Reagan's **star wars** (the Strategic Defense Initiative) – seeks to maintain the posture that nuclear weapons are in some way 'normal' and provisions can be made to treat them in a normal manner. As Secretary of Defense Caspar Weinberger envisages it, the result of such a war must be one in which 'US nuclear capabilities must prevail' and in which the 'termination of hostilities' must be on 'terms favorable to the US and its allies'. There is also built into war-fighting and its theories of 'limited' war the curious belief, concomitant perhaps with a national concept of 'Manifest Destiny', that the Soviets will somehow fit in with US plans. It is unlikely that the rival doctrine of international socialist revolution will so easily accede to US planning. As retired US General Arthur S. Collins has put it (*The Washington Quarterly*, 1983) 'Most of those who postulate scenarios for tactical nuclear war have a faculty for describing situations in which understanding, cooperation and compliance by the enemy make those scenarios credible. There is an unwarranted assumption that compliance will be forthcoming.' As the general adds, all the evidence underlines the fact that however 'careful and discrete' is the first use of nuclear weapons, the response will be 'sudden and massive'.

See also **balance of terror**

wargame to experiment with a variety of putative 'battles', 'attacks', 'nuclear strikes' and similar scenarios, with the intention of developing and elaborating a strategy that might have to be tested in a shooting war. Wargames such as the US's 'Big Stick' or 'Ivy League' can take several days to complete, capitalise on sophisticated computer programs, and attempt to take all the plans and theories into as near as possible a 'real-life' representation, from the first report of out-of-the-ordinary hostile troop movements to the all-out exchanges of **spasm war**.

wargasm term coined by Herman Kahn in a series of briefings delivered to the US military in the late 1950s 'in which some war-plan proposals were referred to as "orgastic spasms of destruction". During one of these briefings I said to the audience "You people do not have a war-plan, you have a wargasm". These expressions were put forward with no particular reference to their sexual implications, but some of my colleagues, more conversant with Freudian concepts . . . than I, argue that the term "spasm war" is more accurate and descriptive than one might think.'

weapons system the military equivalent of the machine – a weapons platform (ship, plane, etc.), a weapon (gun, missile, etc.) and a means of command and communication – plus the human support – scientists to invent, engineers to maintain and service, soldiers to use, workers to build, etc. A concept developed by the USAF in the 1950s as a deliberate parallel to civilian 'management systems'.

weathercock the tendency of a missile (or an aircraft) to turn slightly in the same direction as the wind.

white suits the civilian employees of a contractor who work on a military airbase or similar establishment to service the hardware supplied to the military by that contractor.

window
See **chaff**

window of vulnerability term coined by General Edward Rowney, the Joint Chiefs of Staff representative at the **SALT II** talks in 1980. The result of the agreement reached between Carter and Brezhnev with constraints on missile launchers and a freeze on warheads per type of missile was that the Russians emerged with an approximate 5:2 advantage in **ICBM**s and in ballistic missile **throw-weight**. To the general this meant an unacceptable strategic imbalance and potential vulnerability for the US. Rowney, whose coinage was seized upon by right-wing critics of SALT II, later joined the Reagan Presidential Campaign as a foreign policy adviser. The concept of a window of vulnerability, through which Soviet missiles, with their greater numbers, could strike at the US, was dismissed in 1983 by the Presidential Commission on Strategic Forces, under Congressman Brent Scowcroft. However, while this did reject a principle dear to the President, it was balanced by the need to find a logic for its support for the basing of the **MX** missile in fixed silos until the **Midgetman** missile could be developed; while the committee did reject the 'window of vulnerability', they could hardly put missiles into silos if those silos were genuinely vulnerable to Soviet ICBMs.

WISC acronym for warning system controller. An officer at the **SAC** HQ at Offutt Air Force Base who keeps in constant touch with **NORAD** and who watches two video screens, either of which can track the path of incoming missiles on an outline map of the US.

withhold target a reserve nuclear target, not to be attacked unless specifically indicated. Withhold targets often include major enemy command and control centres, as well as cities. The principle behind reserving such targets is to deliver a strictly **counterforce** first strike, then to threaten one's enemy with more of the same, this time on civilian targets, if there is not immediate surrender. Such US-developed beliefs, in the face of what is known of Soviet doctrines as regards reacting to any form of nuclear attack (absolute **retaliation**, no limited counter-attack) are unlikely to hold up in a real war; it is equally unlikely that such discrete and specific attacks would be made by either side in either first or retaliatory strikes.
See also **ICBM**

wooden bomb the hypothetical concept of an ideal weapon – 100 per cent reliable, carrying an infinite shelf life, requiring no special storage, surveillance or maintenance.

woodpecker the alleged development by Soviet scientists some time since 1977 of a high-powered radar beam that follows the earth's curvature and thus removes the attacking bombers' advantage of being able to fly 'under the radar'.
See also **OTH radar, OTH-B radar**

WWMCCS (*or* WIMEX) acronym for Worldwide Military Command and Control Systems. The command and control arm of **C³I** which links the National Command Authority (NCA, the President and the Secretary of Defense) to the National Military Command System, which executes instructions from the NCA, through channels of command and control, through to the strategic and tactical forces. This segment of WWMCCS comprises the National Military Command Centre in the Pentagon (the 'War Room'), the Alternate National Military Command Centre (in an underground hardened bunker near Fort Richie, Maryland) and the National Emergency Airborne Command Post (the **Kneecap**). All these command centres receive, assess and issue commands based upon information from **NORAD**, which has the overall task of looking constantly for any hostile missile or bomber attacks.

These elements of WWMCCS are themselves linked by the Defense Communications System (DCS) and the Minimum Essential Emergency Communication Network (**MEECN**). The DCS embraces: the Automatic Voice Network (a global telephone network); Automatic Secure Voice Communications (a more sophisticated network, supposedly immune to enemy intercepts); the Automatic Digital Network (AUTODIN), which allows interaction among the various military computers and which is soon to allow dynamic sharing of communications satellite channels among a number of widely dispersed earth stations – the Defense Satellite Communications System (DSCS), the Pentagon's principal military satellite network, some six spacecraft in geosynchronous orbit, with two spares in orbit, which provide super-high frequency (SHF) communications and very fast transmission of data. The current DSCS-2 satellites are being replaced by new DSCS-3 satellites, hardened against nuclear effects and good for ten years in space, rather than DSCS-2's three-year life. The new satellite will include anti-jamming features and a massive increase in manoeuvring flexibility.

Despite the apparent excellence of the WWMCCS, its computers have proved themselves as vulnerable to failure as have the surveillance systems at NORAD. The system was used to overlook and respond to a variety of international crises – the Arab–Israeli war of 1967, the attacks on the USS Pueblo in 1968 and on an EC-121 in 1969 – and on each occasion there were revealed serious and potentially disastrous flaws. In response to severe Congressional criticism, the new Secretary of Defense David Packard set about reforming WWMCCS in 1969, but despite his 'crusade' to iron out the flaws, that lasted until his resignation in 1971, he left a system still far from perfect. The worst error was the ordering of a set of Honeywell computers, designed to link the twenty-six global WWMCCS centres. Late in installation, vastly over-budget, the system soon proved itself quite unsuited to its military duties. By computer standards the system was a full generation behind developments in the private sector. After the 1980 war game 'Proud Spirit', in which a major failure of the WWMCCS computer left Pentagon commanders bereft of vital information at the height of the simulated crisis, one participant said simply 'WIMEX just fell on its ass.' A House Government Operations Committee stated more politely but equally bluntly that due to the excessive complexity of the WWMCCS structure it lacked all real cohesion and as such the program 'is unresponsive to stated requirements; is unreliable; lacks economical and effective growth potential; is incapable of transferring data and information efficiently; makes the exploitation of [automatic data processing] technology extremely difficult and costly; and impairs each command's operation backup capability'. Looked at from a civilian point of view, it would appear that the WWMCCS, the very system designed to maximise the efficiency of the US military war effort, is precisely the one most likely to plunge the US, and the world with it, into a disaster from which there will be no return.

See also **Kneecap, Looking Glass**

Y

yellowcake uranium oxide, used in the manufacture of nuclear weapons.

yield the force of a nuclear explosion, expressed in terms of the amount of TNT (usually as kilotons – thousands of tons – or megatons – millions of tons) that would have been required to create the same explosion.

yield-to-weight ratio the assessment of the force of a nuclear explosion by comparing the force of the explosion to the size of the bomb.

See also **yield**

Z

Z zones in 1958 the UK government issued details of 'the provisional scheme for the control of the public under fallout conditions'. Belts of radioactivity following a nuclear explosion were divided into W, X, Y and Z zones, with the radiation increasing in intensity in each successive zone and the possibility of survival, shelter or rescue becoming decreasingly likely. In an all-out attack on the UK, Z zones will include the destroyed urban centres, which are generally known to have been 'written off' by those who assess the chances of existence for anyone after a nuclear war.

zero option the concept of the *Null-Losung*, the 'zero solution', was first mooted by W. German Chancellor Helmut Schmidt early in 1981. Quite simply he suggested that, were the Russians to remove their long-range SS-4, SS-5 and SS-20 missiles from their Euro-strategic bases, then the US would have no need to proceed with their contentious plans to oppose those missiles with the new Pershing IIs and Tomahawks (**cruise missiles**). Designed primarily to appeal to his own electorate and to the warring factions of his Social Democratic Party, the proposal, highly popular in Europe, was deplored by Washington where it was decreed that only pacifists, neutralists and CND supporters could espouse such a plan. Visiting Germany, Alexander Haig called 'ludicrous' the idea of modifying the nuclear *status quo*; the press took this to be an attack on Schmidt's proposal. Leaving the country Haig attempted to mollify the Germans, explaining that the US had not rejected 'zero option', but merely felt it was over-optimistic as a target. By November 1981 Washington had changed its mind. Zero was acceptable; the problem was to choose absolute zero or the modified zero plus. The Pentagon's Richard Perle opted for absolute zero – the dismantling of all Soviet long-range missiles for the exclusion of the new US weapons from Europe

– while the State Department preferred zero-plus – a more realistic concept given the two sides' ambitions, and one which assumed realistically that some missiles must be deployed in Europe, come what may. President Reagan, acutely aware of the propaganda advantage of so apparently simple an offer, went for absolute zero. He announced the proposal in a speech on 18 November 1981: the US would cancel deployment of 464 Tomahawks and 108 Pershing IIs if the Soviets removed their array of 600 SS-4, SS-5 and SS-20 missiles. This demand included those missiles positioned in the Soviet Far East.

The reaction in both the US and Europe to Reagan's speech was initially good, but critics complained that the delicate issues of arms reduction had been reduced to 'a propaganda treadmill'. Almost as soon as the speech was over, Washington began preparing fallback positions. The Russians, unsurprisingly, rejected zero out of hand. As ever, their mathematics told a very different story to that of the Pentagon. Throughout the Intermediate-range Nuclear Forces Talks (**INF**, formerly Theatre Nuclear Forces, **Talks**) of 1982 and 1983 the two sides bickered without solution. In Washington the opponents of absolute zero stressed the potential horrors of **decoupling** were it to become fact. Ignoring the thousands of theatre weapons already on site, and the proportion of strategic weapons earmarked for the defence of Europe, they claimed that without Tomahawk and Pershing, Europe would be naked, the US would have deserted NATO, the alliance would be destroyed. By January 1983 the President was notably softer on zero: in a speech of 20 January he stressed that the zero option was a fine ideal, but perhaps unattainable. On 30 March he offered an 'interim agreement that would substantially reduce [the missiles] to equal level on both sides'. In short, after eighteen months of the zero or nothing option, Reagan had turned to zero plus; no missiles at all would be perfect, some missiles would still be acceptable. The Soviets rejected the 'interim' plan at once. The INF talks dragged on inconclusively through 1983. On 1 September they were considerably soured by the shooting down of the Korean airliner over Russia. By November the Russians were threatening to walk out. On 14 November the first sixteen Tomahawks arrived in the UK; on 23 November the first nine Pershing IIs were deployed in W. Germany. That day was the end of the talks; the Russians left as promised. The INF talks were over and with them the zero option – a superb piece of propaganda but, in the event, like so many politically opportunistic spectaculars, a hollow gesture.

BIBLIOGRAPHY

Aldridge, Robert C., *First Strike! The Pentagon's Strategy for Nuclear War*, Pluto Press, London, 1983.
AMBIO (The Royal Swedish Academy of Sciences), *Nuclear War: The Aftermath*, Pergamon Press, Oxford, 1983.
British Medical Association, *The Medical Effects of Nuclear War*, John Wiley & Sons, Chichester, 1983.
Brodie, Bernard, *The Absolute Weapon*, 1946.
Campbell, Christy, *War Facts Now*, Fontana Paperbacks, London, 1982.
Campbell, Duncan, *War Plan UK*, Paladin Books, London, 1983.
Cockburn, Andrew, *The Threat: Inside the Russian Military Machine*, New English Library, London, 1985.
Dando, Malcolm and Rogers, Paul, *The Death of Deterrence*, CND Publications, London, 1984.
Delf, George, *Humanizing Hell! Nuclear Weapons and the Law*, Hamish Hamilton, London, 1985.
Ehrlich, Paul R., Sagan, Carl, Kennedy, Donald and Roberts, Walter Orr, *The Nuclear Winter: The World After Nuclear War*, Sidgwick & Jackson, London, 1985.
Ford, Daniel, *The Button: The Nuclear Trigger – Does It Work*, George Allen & Unwin, London, 1985.
Freedman, Lawrence, *Britain and Nuclear Weapons*, Macmillan Press, London, 1980.
Goodwin, Peter, *Nuclear War: The Facts*, Macmillan, London, 1982.
Green, Jonathon, *Newspeak: A Dictionary of Jargon*, Routledge & Kegan Paul, London, 1983.
Gunston, Bill, *Jane's Dictionary of Aerospace Terms*, MacDonald and Jane's, London, 1980.
Haldeman, H. R. and Dimona, Joseph, *The Ends of Power*, Dell, New York, 1978.
Hayward, Brigadier P. C. H. (ed.), *Jane's Dictionary of Military Terms*, MacDonald and Jane's, London, 1975.
Hilgartner, Stephen, Bell, Richard C. and O'Connor, Rory, *Nukespeak: The Selling of Nuclear Technology in America*, Sierra Club Books, San Francisco, 1982.
Howe, Russell Warren, *Weapons: The International Game of Arms, Money and Diplomacy*, Abacus Books, London, 1981.
Kahn, Herman, *Thinking About the Unthinkable*, Weidenfeld & Nicolson, London, 1962.

Kahn, Herman, *On Escalation*, The Pall Mall Press, London, 1965.

Kaldor, Mary, *The Baroque Arsenal*, Andre Deutsch, London, 1982.

Kaplan, Donald M. and Schwerner, Armand, *The Domesday Dictionary*, Jonathan Cape, London, 1964.

Karas, Thomas, *The New High Ground: Systems and Weapons of Space Age War*, New English Library, London, 1983.

Lee, Christopher, *The Final Decade: Will We Survive the 1980s?*, Sphere Books, London, 1983.

Osgood, Charles E., *An Alternative to War or Surrender*, University of Illinois Press, Urbana, Ill., 1962.

Pretz, Bernhard, *A Dictionary of Military and Technological Abbreviations and Acronyms*, Routledge & Kegan Paul, London, 1983.

Pringle, Peter and Arkin, William, *SIOP: Nuclear Wars from the Inside*, Sphere Books, London, 1983.

Pringle, Peter and Spiegelman, James, *The Nuclear Barons*, Michael Joseph, London, 1982.

Rogers, Paul, *Guide to Nuclear Weapons 1984–85*, University of Bradford School of Peace, Bradford, 1984.

Safire, William, *Safire's Political Dictionary*, Ballantine Books, New York, 1980.

Stevenson, Michael and Weal, John, *Nuclear Dictionary*, Longman, London, 1985.

Talbott, Strobe, *Deadly Gambits: The Reagan Administration and the Stalemate in Nuclear Arms Control*, Pan Books, London, 1985.

Wilson, Andrew, *The Disarmer's Handbook of Military Technology and Organization*, Penguin Books, Harmondsworth, 1983.

York, Herbert, *The Race to Oblivion*, Simon & Schuster, New York, 1970.

Zuckermann, Lord, *Nuclear Illusion and Reality*, Collins, London, 1982.